Dear Jeff,
We are looking forward
to doing much business with
you.
Miles Away gives you an idea
of what we do not due and
hopefully where we stand —

Enjoy the read.

All the best,

MILES AWAY...
WORLDS APART

Empowering Lessons Gleaned From
Experiences of a Whistleblower

selflessness generosity integrity
goodness sincerity kindness
friendship leadership responsibility
sensitivity faith community
charity respect

MILES AWAY...
WORLDS APART

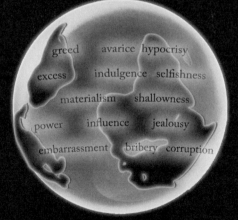

greed avarice hypocrisy
excess indulgence selfishness
materialism shallowness
power influence jealousy
embarrassment bribery corruption

Alan Sakowitz

Published in 2010 by
Legacy Series Press, LLC
1111 Kane Concourse, Suite 401F
Bay Harbor Islands, Florida 33154
www.legacyseriespress.com

ISBN 978-0-615-38240-1

Cover design: Amy M. Crawford
Interior text design and typesetting: Daniel Crack

Dedicated to my beloved wife

Leah

the source of my inspiration
and the center of my world

Table of Contents

Author's Note

The neighbors I write about live or have lived within six blocks of my home. Almost all of my neighbors referred to in the community stories are also my friends, many of them close friends. Some of the people moved from the community before I had the opportunity to meet them, but all of them had an impact on helping the community of North Miami Beach become a caring, nurturing environment.

Prologue

Common sense is very uncommon.

~Horace Greeley

S A REAL ESTATE DEVELOPER, I regularly receive phone calls about land available for development, distressed properties at rock bottom prices, and commercial mortgages for sale from banks. When *Miguel*,[1] one of the real estate brokers with whom I work, called me one sunny morning in early August 2009, he mentioned that through another broker he had learned of a prominent South Florida law firm that had won several significant settlements for its clients. Miguel explained that the settlements called for a stream of payments, while the firm's clients wanted lump sum payouts. He asked if I would be interested in buying the funded settlement agreements. I mentioned that if the risk were low and the return reasonable, I would be interested in learning more.

At the time, I could not have imagined that in a week I would begin a surreal adventure just for agreeing to "learn more," an eighty-four-day ride through an exciting, terrifying, intense drama involving

---

1 To protect the identity of certain individuals who appear in this book, names have been changed and are italicized when they first appear.

the largest fraud in the history of South Florida, and I would witness greed and its blinding powers in truly stunning ways, as well as the dangerous collusion between business and politics.

Hours of meetings brought me face to face with a spiky-haired, immensely charismatic man named Scott Rothstein who had created a culture of corruption. I would come to the inescapable conclusion that, for the good of the public, he had to be stopped. Honorable people were taken in and became casualties of this culture of greed. Its magnetic attraction was too strong for a great many otherwise reasonable people. It was difficult to determine whether the political leaders and the law enforcement personnel were owned by this master manipulator, but it certainly appeared as if many were. Choosing the wrong individuals and authorities to whom to report this well-concocted plan of deceit, deception, and corruption could have been deadly.

Yet I felt that I had no choice. The man had to be stopped.

The fact is, if Scott Rothstein ruined just his own life, it would be a tragedy. But he did more; he created the occasion for decent people to destroy their own lives and those of their families and friends. For that reason, the impact of the catastrophe is enormous, and the array of losses includes money, property, licenses to practice law, reputations, liberty, and likely even life itself. The community and the country also suffered, since the impression created by Rothstein's dealings was that everyone and everything was for sale at a price, including law enforcement and government leaders.

Because of the ease with which so many became Rothstein's willing victims or co-conspirators, looking deep into what occurred, and how it can be prevented in the future, is essential. Lessons learned from the Rothstein debacle, if taken to heart, can prevent others from falling prey to similar fraudsters or people whose condition borders on sociopathy.

At the same time, looking at a world that is the antithesis of Rothstein's palace of deceit is also important to examine, for doing so provides a real choice about what it means to live a truly fulfilling life. You see, just sixteen miles from Rothstein's world is a totally different world, a community that straddles a city named North Miami Beach, where wealth and fulfillment is not measured in dollars, but in deeds. This book compares these two worlds that, though geographically close, are philosophically light years apart.

Every person becomes who he is by the choices he makes. For each of us, there are a number of forks in the road, and each time we encounter one of them we need to choose the direction we will head. These forks in the road arise at different times and frequencies for each of us, but no one passes through life without reaching them. The better our past selections as we headed down the road, the easier it is for us to make good choices among the alternatives each time we are faced with a new choice. This book is written with the hope that describing the two vastly different approaches to a meaningful life will prepare the reader to make better choices when reaching his or her own fork in the road. For the vast majority, it will be confirmation that the right path was chosen. For anyone who, like Rothstein, is headed in the wrong direction, it offers words of caution, guidance, and an alternative.

With G-d's help, this message will reach at least one person who can be persuaded to choose a better and more meaningful way to spend his years on Earth. If such a change can be brought about in that one person's life path, this book was worth writing. If *more* than one reader gains, then to me, this book will be a *major* success.

selflessness generosity integrity
goodness sincerity kindness
friendship leadership responsibility
sensitivity faith community
charity respect

greed avarice hypocrisy
excess indulgence selfishness
materialism shallowness
power influence jealousy
embarrassment bribery corruption

Chapter 1

Meeting the Chairman

*Outside show is a poor substitute
for inner worth.*

~AESOP

M Y TERRIFYING, surreal adventure began a week after Miguel's phone call, around August 4, 2009, when I heard that my business partner of over fifteen years, Maurice Egozi, was also meeting with Miguel. Maurice called to see when I would be available. Our meeting was to be with the chairman of the as yet undisclosed "prominent" law firm. Maurice had met with *Akbar*, a real estate associate with R.L. Pearson and Associates, Inc. (RL Pearson), a real estate development company and broker who claimed to be the exclusive broker for the law firm selling the settlement agreements. Maurice wanted me to know that Akbar insisted that we sign a three-page non-disclosure agreement, which is a document that is often signed before a purchase or other opportunity is presented to a purchaser or investor. It prevents the prospective purchaser or investor from disclosing any of the information, which is generally extremely confidential, about the opportunity to a third party. Signing the agreement, Maurice said, was a prerequisite to Akbar informing us of the name and location of the law firm, and providing us with a forty-seven-page, classified business plan explaining the settlement funding opportunity.

When Maurice informed Akbar that he would not sign the non-disclosure agreement until I reviewed it, Akbar was somewhat concerned to learn I was an attorney. Akbar insisted that the only item he could provide without the signed non-disclosure agreement was the latest list of settlement agreements available for sale with their prices and returns.

After insisting that nothing could be divulged without the non-disclosure agreement signed, Akbar nevertheless handed Maurice the forty-seven-page confidential business plan. Maurice shared the plan and the list of available settlement agreements with me. I reviewed the documents in detail and had many questions. It seemed the plan was only intended for perusal, not serious review. My first thought was, *Why would anyone buy an investment based on a business plan in which all of the pertinent information is redacted?* (Redacting a document means to black out all of the identifying information, such as names and addresses.)

Even though we hadn't signed the non-disclosure agreement, Akbar just could not resist giving us the name of the "prominent" law firm: Rothstein, Rosenfeldt and Adler, P.A., more commonly known as RRA. We were not familiar with the firm, which had over seventy attorneys and 150 people on staff, including secretaries, paralegals, bookkeepers, and other personnel. Its main office was at 401 East Las Olas Blvd. Ft. Lauderdale, Florida, approximately sixteen miles away from my own community in North Miami Beach, Florida. Coincidentally, we were told, R.L. Pearson's office was in the same building, four floors below.

I drove to Fort Lauderdale where Miguel and Maurice, accompanied by Akbar, were already waiting for me outside the building. We thought we were going to look at investments but we soon found out that, instead, we were given front-row seats to one of the most bizarre and alluring situations we would probably ever encounter, a situation that was like nothing we could have expected, and nothing for which we could have been prepared.

Before going up to meet Chairman Rothstein we went to the 12th floor and met with Richard L. Pearson. Pearson explained that he had become the exclusive broker when a hedge fund that had been funding many of the prior settlements ran into financial problems and could not be investing in new settlements. Pearson wanted twenty percent of our profits; he felt it was a fair amount for providing us with an opportunity that paid over 100 percent per annum with virtually no risk. Just hearing those words "100 percent per annum" and "virtually no risk" raised a big red flag for me – for what should be, but are often not, obvious reasons.

Rule #1 in investing is that you don't make a return of 100 percent per year on a passive investment (one in which you do absolutely nothing but invest money) without a considerable amount of risk. The details of the proposal meant that we would actually be receiving 207 percent per annum return on our money. This sent the red flag even higher, and further review increased my confusion and disbelief. For example, the third page of the confidential settlement funding business plan stated the following:

'… "purchase opportunity" An opportunity exists for a purchaser to secure a minimum of 20% by funding a one-time lump sum discounted cash advance to individual plaintiffs who have fully settled their employment-related claims mainly sexual harassment and whistleblower cases[2] and who would otherwise receive their settlement amount paid over a period of time. The advantage to plaintiff would be in the immediate receipt of a one-time lump sum payment, with the purchaser being assigned the right to receive the settlement amount over the payment term agreed upon by the defendant. The purchaser's lump sum payment would be secured by an assignment of proceeds of the full settlement amount which

---

2 A whistleblower is an informant who exposes wrongdoing within an organization in the hope of stopping it.

would have been deposited in a trust account established by
the plaintiff's attorney prior to the purchase being made by the
purchaser. The purchaser would receive the secure payment from
the attorney's trust account over a period of months, generally
3–12 months, resulting in a minimum 20% return.'

In legal terms, an "assignment" is the transfer to another of one's
right to receive something, such as money or services, under a
contract. Other than in certain limited situations or in certain types
of contracts, assignments are perfectly legal. In fact, most types of
contracts and rights are freely assignable as a matter of law, without
the necessity of language expressly permitting assignment. Therefore,
it is not uncommon for attorneys to insert, in certain legal docu-
ments, a provision prohibiting assignment or other transfer.

From the above-quoted description it sounded like the return
would be around twenty percent, and that payments would be over
a period of as long as twelve months. The list of available settlements
for sale told a different story. In particular, we noticed that the list
included three $900,000 settlements that could be purchased for
$660,000 each, which constituted a $240,000 discount per settle-
ment. The settlement provided for three monthly payments of
$300,000 each. That was a thirty-six percent discount, which was
certainly alluring. At the same time, we couldn't help but wonder
why a plaintiff would sell a stream of $300,000 per month for three
months at such a steep discount. The actual return was 207 percent
per annum.

Reading the document, I thought, *Not bad for minimal risk, but
perhaps too good to be true!* Then it was time to meet the chairman.
We took the elevator of the elegant building to the penthouse on
the 16th floor and entered it to find an off-duty, uniformed Fort
Lauderdale police officer guarding the private side door to Scott
Rothstein's office through which we entered. The huge office had
all the accoutrements of success, with a breathtaking view of the
Atlantic Ocean. From looking at the walls, one could see what a

well-connected attorney Scott Rothstein was. Everybody who was anybody in the world of politics, sports, entertainment, or philanthropy appeared in a framed, autographed photograph with Mr. Rothstein. Thank-you note after thank-you note was framed and hanging on the wall, acknowledging the generosity of Mr. Rothstein – apparently one of Fort Lauderdale's most philanthropic individuals. Everything on the wall was positioned as a trophy, including a photograph of Rothstein's wife holding six shopping bags from expensive stores.

Rothstein's enormous desk had a sign that read, "A good lawyer knows the law. A great lawyer knows the judges." It didn't take long for us to hear from Mr. Rothstein himself how well he knew the judges, or his role in getting them appointed to the bench. Behind the desk were a computer and four monitors. The setting alone was a draw for attracting investors. Everything about Scott Rothstein and his office spelled success and influence.

Prominently displayed on Rothstein's desk were the Five Books of Moses – the holy Torah, the basis of Jewish law. This ostentatious display of the foundation of Jewish law bespoke a level of moral hypocrisy that would later come to my mind on repeated occasions.

After I sat down on his alligator-skin couch, I took a good look at Rothstein, who appeared to be in his forties. He was on the short side with dark, spiked hair, and he wore an exceedingly handsome suit, one that I assumed was custom-made. Grabbing a Diet Coke in an old-fashioned nickel bottle, Rothstein began telling us about himself, stopping from time to time to enjoy a gulp of the soft drink. In case we hadn't heard or read about his generosity, Rothstein spent quite a while acquainting us with some of the larger donations he and his firm had recently made to neighborhood charities, including religious institutions, hospitals, and organizations that helped disadvantaged children. He gave a million here and half a million there.

Rothstein expounded upon his vast political connections. He enjoyed telling us how many times Florida Governor Charlie Crist and former presidential candidate John McCain had visited his house. In case we were not yet impressed, he stated that he was often on the phone with Governor Crist as many as five times a day. "I am one of Crist's closest friends," Rothstein announced.

Maurice and I could not help but wonder what the connection was between the hundreds of thousands of dollars Rothstein raised for the governor and the "goodies" he said he received from him. We did not have to speculate for long. Rothstein was proud to tell us that judges get appointed when he gives the word. The appointment of city and county commissioners was no different. Rothstein mentioned that when a commissioner was recently suspended after being charged with corruption, he selected the replacement. *No wonder*, I thought, *that Fort Lauderdale was nicknamed "Fraud Lauderdale."*

As we were talking, I glanced at a picture of California Governor Arnold Schwarzenegger in a bathrobe with a nice note to Rothstein. The picture itself begged for an explanation. Rothstein leaned back and smiled as if each picture represented a great story about a long-time and close friend. Rothstein had raised $500,000 for Governor Schwarzenegger, half of it coming from RRA. By this point no one would have been surprised to learn that his "friends" were a never-ending source of referrals of government and corporate business. It was understood that he needed to keep supporting them as well.

As if there were any need to further convince us that he was the man to know in Broward County, Rothstein elaborated on his connections to law enforcement, such as his connection to Sheriff Al Lamberti, for whose campaign, we later learned, he had raised $260,000. After a few more war stories, Rothstein must have satisfied himself that we were properly charmed and, as he began to walk around the room, the ostentatiously successful, politically influential philanthropist disappeared and he began to speak about his calling as a lawyer: punishing employers who abused their female staff. Nothing, he said, bothered him more. He did whatever it took to get justice for those poor, mistreated victims.

Losing these cases was not an option, he continued. His clients counted on him and he delivered in a ruthless, no-holds-barred way. His team was complete with dozens of former law enforcement officers sporting the most sophisticated surveillance equipment found anywhere. Rothstein proudly and loudly proclaimed that he could hear a conversation a block away with his eavesdropping devices and that his team routinely videotaped the scum-of-the-earth employers in compromising positions mistreating his poor, defenseless clients. Terrified of his larger-than-life image, major companies that found themselves on the defensive side of a Rothstein lawsuit, flocked to hire his firm as a consultant. This, they calculated, presented Rothstein and his firm with a conflict of interest, thereby preventing him from representing clients against them ever again – or at least as long as they retained him as a consultant.

During this act of the performance, the impression Rothstein projected was that of a tireless advocate for the harassed. He had become so successful, he told us, and had won so many settlements, that a niche market had emerged. RRA's clients wanted lump sum payments at settlement, and the perpetrators who abused RRA's clients didn't mind depositing all the settlement proceeds upfront in RRA's trust account, but they wanted the payments disbursed to Rothstein's clients on a monthly basis, generally over a period of three-to-eight months. The settlements were required by their terms to be kept confidential because the employer's reprehensible conduct was not something the employer wanted to become known to the public. Spreading out the payments, the defendants reasoned, was a good way to keep the plaintiffs' mouths shut. Oh, Rothstein was no ordinary lawyer! He was a genius. No lawyer was his match, or so he wanted us to believe. His untrammeled ego knew no bounds.

Typically, an abusive employer and RRA's client signed a ten-page settlement agreement to resolve the dispute and keep it strictly and completely confidential. The settlement agreements didn't provide that the settlement proceeds couldn't be sold or transferred. Therefore, they were freely assignable; such was the magic formula that allowed both the employer and the employee to be satisfied. The employer wired the settlement proceeds into RRA's trust account, knowing that if the employee breached the confidentiality of the settlement, the employer could go to court and block the disbursement of the remaining proceeds. Well, it wasn't quite that simple. Rothstein said it had never happened in the seven years that his clients had been assigning their proceeds. The plan was practically foolproof. After all, what employer would go to court and announce to the world that he was caught in a compromising position with an employee and had entered into a confidential settlement agreement after which the employee then told someone?

However, Rothstein explained that if an employee did breach the confidentiality agreement and the employer did go to court, RRA would represent the investor for free. Maurice asked if that was a conflict of interest since RRA was also representing the employee.

Without missing a beat, Rothstein replied, "No."

I almost rolled my eyes.

In any case, Rothstein said, the mere filing of a lawsuit was not enough to stop the payments. Rothstein continued making the payments until he received a court order to stop. That was the only risk in investing in the "confidential settlement agreements." If Rothstein was correct, up until now not a single payment had ever been missed on any settlement agreement. That made the risk pretty low. Nonetheless, if a person were to invest in only one settlement agreement, and the employee then breached the confidentiality provision, the investor would face a substantial loss. If numerous agreements were purchased and there was only one breach, the loss would be minimal and manageable.

Since the settlement agreements did not prohibit an assignment of the settlement proceeds, Rothstein devised a plan of allowing the employee to assign the proceeds to an investor. The investor deposited the discounted cash settlement amount, which was then disbursed to the employee. The investor received the stream of payments from the defendant-employer. According to Rothstein, the employer wired the entire settlement amount into RRA's trust account at TD Bank, a well-respected bank in Broward. The employee assigned his or her interest in the settlement agreement to an investor for a discounted amount. The employee received the cash immediately and the investor received the monthly payout.

A law firm's trust account is a bank account into which money is deposited for payment or possible payment to other parties. For example, if the money is for the purchase of a home and the home is actually purchased, the deposit money is paid by the law firm to the seller of the home. If the money is for the settlement of a legal dispute, most of the money is paid to the injured party, with the law firm possibly deducting its legal fee and paying that amount into its operating account. The bottom line is that most money deposited in a law firm's trust account does not actually belong to the law firm.

Maurice and I looked at the available settlements to purchase and the ones that caught our attention were the "660" ones. These involved the payment of $660,000 by the investor to the employee for the assignment of his or her proceeds. The employee would immediately be paid the $660,000, and the investor would receive the settlement proceeds of $900,000 paid in equal payments over a period of three months. That was a thirty-six percent discount but a 207 percent per annum profit. In two months we surmised that most of our money would be returned ($600,000 out of $660,000). In the last month, we would receive the remaining $60,000 of our investment with a $240,000 profit. It's better than working. It doesn't get any better than that, we thought!

"Oh, I forgot to tell you – the reason we had to keep this little business on the Q.T.," added Chairman Rothstein, "was that none of the defense lawyers realized that the settlement agreements didn't say they were not assignable." If word got out, the defense attorneys would make all future settlement agreements non-assignable. As an "honest" attorney, Rothstein would not be able to facilitate the transactions and everyone would lose. No more investors would be needed. Again, Rothstein repeated that the only risk of losing was if the employee breached the confidentiality clause and the employer filed suit and won. Unless an injunction was entered, Rothstein kept disbursing the proceeds from RRA's trust account. The bonus of working with RRA was that, if a suit were to be filed, RRA would rigorously represent investors at no charge.

At about this point in Rothstein's pitch, most potential investors quickly eliminated the word "potential" from their description as a "potential investor." Their only question was, "Where do we wire the money?"

Maurice and I, however, noticed the field of red flags.

To begin with, nine of the eighteen settlement agreements available for sale had been sold. We wondered why someone would purchase a settlement at a twenty-six percent discount payable over six months, and one at a thirty-eight percent discount payable over eight months, leaving the ones with payments over only three months and a thirty-six percent discount still available. I understood why the one with a twenty-seven percent discount payable over eight months was available and the one at a thirty-three percent discount payable over ten months was available, but for the life of me I couldn't figure out why better ones were available and worse ones had been sold. There was no other information available that could be used to evaluate the worth or risk of a settlement, so the only criteria with which to select a settlement agreement to purchase were the discount and the length of the payout period.

Next, I had to assume that every defense lawyer involved with sexual harassment and qui tam cases (cases also known as whistleblower cases in which any person having knowledge of violations of federal law may bring an action in federal district court under the False Claims Act on behalf of himself and the United States government, and share in any recovery) had failed to realize that the anti-assignment clause was missing. Then, I had to assume that most of the investors were too unsophisticated to figure out which investments paid the best returns.

Could it be, I wondered, *that these attorneys were all inexperienced, sloppy or just plain stupid and that these investors were the ones who never did well in math?* The next concern I had was: "Why was the yield over 100 percent per annum, and in some cases over 200 percent?" That led us to another warning signal: why would the employees sell their settlement agreements at such substantial discounts?

I addressed my concerns to Rothstein. With a straight face, he leaned toward me and the legs of his custom-made trousers rose ever so slightly, revealing a revolver on his left ankle. I did not think this change of position was deliberate, but others said to me later that every word and every movement of Rothstein's was calculated. Regardless, it made an impression on me.

"Alan," Rothstein said. "You do not get it. Some of my clients do not have the money to pay the rent, put food on their table, or fill their car with gas."

"Fair enough," I responded. "I can understand why they would borrow $10,000 at loan shark rates until their first $300,000 arrived. I can see them being ready to pay $20,000 back in a month for the $10,000 now, but why would they discount the other $890,000?"

"They just want to put the whole nightmare behind them," said Rothstein.

"Okay, so when can we meet your clients?" I asked him.

"You can't," he replied. "It's a violation of the confidentiality agreements."

"You mean all I get to see are the settlement agreements without the benefit of discussing them with your clients?" I asked.

"Well," he said, "I can't let you see the originals, only the redacted copies."

Yeah, right, I thought.

"I would like to speak with the attorneys in your firm who handled the cases," was my response.

"Okay," said Rothstein. "You are speaking with him."

Just then, my broker Miguel said, "Alan, Scott is a reputable attorney. You are talking to him like you don't trust him."

"Miguel," I said. "Let me tell you something. If my investment group makes a purchase, you, Richard, and Akbar are each making a substantial commission even if we lose money. We are not investing a dime until we can figure out whether this is the deal of a lifetime or simply a scam. "Scott," I said, turning to Rothstein, "I'd like to look at your file on this case."

Rising suddenly to his feet and backing up, Rothstein blurted out, "Those are off-limits. They are confidential."

"Wait a second," I said. "I am not asking you to show me files at random. I just want to see your client's file on this case and the settlement agreement. It all relates to the investment we are making. I want to know what we are buying."

After a few more exchanges, we walked out, saying we would think about it and get back to him. We knew it was either the deal of a lifetime or a total scam. There was nothing in between.

Had Rothstein been making his proposal out of the back of a warehouse, I do not think the meeting would have lasted too long at all, and there would not have been a second meeting. But we were in the office of the chairman and CEO of a large, reputable law firm, and that went a long way toward creating an appearance of credibility. *"He has everything to lose and nothing to gain from scamming us,"* we agreed. *Would he risk his entire firm and his reputation by selling settlements that did not exist?*

After our meeting, we headed to Pearson's office. Maurice and I wanted to speak privately, so we asked Akbar, Miguel, and Richard to give us a couple of minutes. We all took the elevator down to the 12th floor, and Maurice and I went to one side as the other three entered Pearson's office. We decided not to say much since we suspected even the hallway might be bugged.

When we entered Pearson's office, Akbar asked me for the signed non-disclosure agreement. The agreement stated that we would not disclose anything we learned after signing the agreement. By now, we had learned about all we were going to learn. I made a couple of changes to the agreement and signed it as changed, although Akbar said it had to be signed "as is" with no changes. They never asked Maurice to sign, so he did not sign. Pearson never counter-signed and did not give me a copy of the one I executed with the changes. I wanted to speak with an attorney and find out if his firm had clients settling cases with RRA's clients, but I could not take a chance of calling attention to the agreements being assigned if it was not widely known. Each time this thought entered my mind, I regretted having signed that agreement. But eventually I did run the facts by an attorney that was not involved in the employment law specialty. I asked Pearson if he knew any of the RRA attorneys well.

He said he had known David Boden for about ten years. "David," he said, "was my attorney many years ago." I do not remember the specifics but since David was only licensed in New York, it may have been that Pearson had lived in New York and David had represented him there. Anyway, Pearson swore by David and he said we could trust him. He gave me David's number. I called him and asked him if Scott Rothstein was for real. David assured me that he was. David admitted that Scott was a bit eccentric, but stated that Scott was honest and easy to do business with.

What was with the office? we wondered. Certainly it was designed to be impressive. But why? Was it a great way to attract business? Was it to satisfy Rothstein's oversized ego? If it was just to attract business or because of his huge ego, then *okay*, I thought, *it is not my taste, but different strokes for different folks.* But if the office was designed to create the perfect setting for a scam, then that was a horse of a different color. It seemed only the external was important to Rothstein. Substance didn't matter. Appearance was everything. "Does he really believe that all of those actors, entertainers, sports stars, politicians, and heads of charitable organizations are his friends?" we asked each other. *Or could it be that he believes that for several million dollars he can create an image that will bring him endless business?*

Rothstein had gone to great effort to create an illusion that he was both successful and respected by all and that his reputation was beyond reproach. But I wasn't impressed. As I drove the sixteen miles home, it dawned on me that North Miami Beach, the community of which I am a member, and Rothstein's lifestyle, were polar opposites. They were miles away but worlds apart. There was nothing in Rothstein's world, it appeared, except Rothstein. Others were only important if they could be of benefit to him in some way or other.

My rabbi, Rabbi Ephraim Eliyahu Shapiro, once explained in a sermon that in Judaism, the right side is considered the prominent side, the more important side. He said this, notwithstanding his being a lefty himself! Rabbi Shapiro said when we put on our trousers, according to Jewish custom, we put our right leg in first. When we put on a shirt, we put our right arm in first. When we wash first thing in the morning, we wash our right hand first. Before we eat bread, we wash the right hand first. When we put on shoes, it's the right shoe that is put on first.

My rabbi then asked, "If the right side is the stronger side, the more important side, then why is the heart on the left side?" He provided a beautiful answer: "Because my heart is not for me, and your heart is not for you. My heart is for you, and your heart is for me. If your heart is for another person and you face that person, your heart is on that person's right side. If we live life always looking to help other people and facing people and seeing what we can do for them, then our heart is always on the right side. And then it is just where it belongs. But if, G-d forbid, we live life always looking to see what we can do for ourselves and we do not care about others, then our heart is on our left side. Our job as human beings is to live with our heart on the right side. That is how we perfect the world."

Hearing this sermon, I realized there were true stories from my neighborhood that were about neighbors helping other neighbors. Every one of the stories I could think of concerned people who lived their lives with their hearts on the right side. After spending an afternoon with Scott Rothstein, there was nothing about him that showed his heart to be on the right side; it seemed that he thought only about the external, the illusion, the appearance; yet I understood that appearance without substance was meaningless.

As I speak of the good deeds of my neighbors and contrast them with Rothstein's world of falsity, opulence, and illusion, my goal is to demonstrate how easy, yet meaningful, it is to make a positive difference and inspire others to make good choices.

Chapter 2

My Community

*In this world it is not what we take up, but
what we give up, that makes us rich.*

~HENRY WARD BEECHER

M
ILES AWAY, WORLDS APART is the best way to
describe the dissimilarity of my community and its
lifestyle, and that of Rothstein's. It doesn't matter to
me that the community I live in is not as aestheti-
cally beautiful as other areas, or that the houses are not necessarily
as large or new as elsewhere. My wife Leah and I felt that it was
an ideal environment in which to raise children, and for our own
personal growth. Just knowing that neighbors were getting up in the
morning addressing the needs of others was enough – figuratively
at least, to change a person's DNA. Our children lived among their
teachers, their principals, and other neighbors who were constantly
engaged in acts of kindness. We believed having such role models to
guide our children would make a lasting impression on them. It was
an environment where children were learning the lessons that we
learned in our own homes: that a life well lived is not measured by
one's material possessions but rather by the amount of help one can
give to others in need.

Allow me to take you on a tour of our community. Our commu-
nity is designed around our religious needs. Our Sabbath, *Shabbos*

as we call it, and holidays are spiritual days in which we do not drive vehicles, turn on electricity, or use telephones, among other things. We, therefore, build our synagogues, or *shuls*, within walking distance of our homes. In our neighborhood we have established seven such *shuls* to accommodate the more than 800 families. Two of the *shuls* are building newer, larger, and more beautiful facilities. We are fortunate to have extraordinary educational institutions as well, including a preschool, boys' day school, girls' day school, boys' middle school, boys' high school/post high school, and two girls' middle school/high schools. Because of the proximity of the schools to the community, these facilities are also used on our holidays and our *Shabbos* to provide a place for children's groups and other ancillary services for the community.

Our community also includes a *kollel*, a learning center that is packed six days and nights a week with adults from the community and beyond who wish to come and learn in pairs or in groups. At the *kollel's* nucleus are ten Torah scholars learning and teaching full time. Those who wish to learn range from the most basic of beginners to the greatest of scholars. Our *kollel* is a crown that we have only recently been able to afford for our community. In this economy, keeping it funded is a huge challenge. Once a week we have father-and-son learning as well. That program has become so successful that it was moved to the boys' high school so everyone could fit into one physical structure.

Our approach to charity includes lending money without charging interest. To fill this need, we have what we call *gemachs*. These are loan societies staffed by volunteers. They include not only a free loan society, in which loans are given to those in need who have the ability to pay the funds back, but also loan societies that have no expectation that the money will be paid back. In the first type, the money is lent without interest. In the second type, the money, too, is lent without interest. But when the loans are made, even though the borrower would like to pay the money back and probably even intends to pay the money back, the society makes the loans, expecting that the borrower will not be able to repay them. It is called a loan society so the dignity of the recipients is not lost.

Our other *gemachs* provide other services. They include a children's *gemach*, in which there is beautiful clothing available for those who don't have the funds or whose funds are limited. There is an adult's *gemach* for clothing. There are two *gemachs* where chairs and tables are lent out for parties and other events, two *gemachs* for books, and two *gemachs* for Torah tapes and CDs. There is a *gemach* that provides for the ritual items one needs in our community during *shivah*, the week of mourning upon the loss of a parent, a sibling, or a child. During that week, meals are also provided by members of the community for the mourners and their families.

We have an organization called *Shmira* (to watch), which provides a level of free patrols in the neighborhood and covers certain hours of the night and is available during the day. That is one layer of our security. The members of *Shmira* also open locks when people are locked out of their homes and provide many other services without charge.

There are several charitable organizations relating to food. One location is a little further away from the community, again so the dignity of the recipient is not taken away. It is a kosher food bank and those who are in need come by appointment, so that others won't see them partaking of the services. There are other arrangements made for kosher meats and other products that are expensive, in which a person goes to a store and picks up an order just like any other customer, except that the cost of his order has been prepaid by the community. Again the person is able to walk in and maintain his dignity. There are other monies given out for all kinds of emergencies. Some people, unfortunately, need the community's help on a regular basis. Others experience a tragedy, lose a job, or have other hardships. These individuals may only need help for a short period of time until they are back on their feet. As hard as our community strives to meet the vital needs of its residents, our community is still a work in progress. We have clearly not been successful in meeting everyone's needs all of the time, especially given the limited resources and the growing numbers of requests for assistance. However, that does not deter us from continuing to try our utmost and to regularly seek more volunteers, innovative programs, and resources.

There are charitable organizations within the community that are so private that I was asked not to publish that they even exist, because those who receive from these charities would never take if the charity was publicly known. It is that level of dignity that the heads of the charities felt was important to maintain. At times, an employer is given extra money to give to an employee when it becomes known that this person needs funds, but will not take charity.

We are taught that the best way to give charity is to give it anonymously. The giver does not know to whom the charity is going and the receiver does not know from whom it came. So there are organizations set up to collect and distribute money in exactly that manner.

We have numerous groups for children. We have *chesed* (kindness) organizations. By kindness I mean in every fashion and in every form. For example, a few years ago a woman in our community was quite sick. For months on end teenagers in the *chesed* organization of one of the girls' schools dressed the woman's children every morning before school, took them rollerblading and bike riding, and did everything for them that their mother would have done if she were not ill. After school these teenage girls arranged to help with homework and make life as meaningful as possible for the children, at least as meaningful as it could be with a parent that is incapacitated.

We also have *Bikur Cholim* (visiting the sick). *Bikur Cholim* helps families when someone is sick, arranges for rides to the hospital when needed, provides meals for families when family members are in the hospital, and provides visitors to those who have no visitors. The organization lends walkers and wheelchairs to those who need them or their visitors. When women give birth, there is another organization that arranges meals for them. And, segueing from birth to life, we have a burial society that provides for the dignified preparation of a body for burial in accordance with the laws of our faith.

This list is incomplete because there are services in our community that I am not even aware of, since so many people like to provide them in a dignified and anonymous fashion. Often the person looking for a particular service doesn't have to come to the one who provides it, since there are those in our community who have a sixth sense of who needs what and make sure the person or family receives it.

On Sunday morning, January 31, 2010, as the clock struck midnight, we added our newest service to the community, *Hatzalah*, which means rescue and relief in Hebrew. It is a volunteer Emergency Medical Service (EMS) organization whose primary mission is to save lives by providing basic life support services in those vital first few minutes of an emergency situation until an ambulance or Fire Rescue arrives. Since *Hatzalah's* well-trained volunteers live and work in the community, the goal is to have an average response time of one-to-three minutes.

Just describing our community does not do it justice. The following story about my neighbor Scott Bugay[3] makes the contrast between Rothstein's world (of greed and self-aggrandizement) and my community, all the more vivid.

All About The Players

Scott Bugay is my next-door neighbor and has managed a team in little league baseball for the last nine years. He has not always had the best players in the league, but his team finished with the top regular season record in seven of the nine seasons. Curious as to what set apart his team I went to a game in his seventh season. Right off the bat, I saw one major difference. Managing a team and paying the sponsorship fee came with the right to name the back of the players' jerseys. Easily, I could guess the business or profession of all but one team. As you could imagine, the shirts read "Jones Plumbing" and "Smith and Jones Law Offices." But even though Scott Bugay is an

3 My neighbors who allowed their names and stories to be used in this book were neither interested in recognition nor in their stories even being known. However, they agreed to allow me to include their stories so that the cumulative effect of so many beautiful anecdotes could inspire others, and so that readers would know the stories are real.

attorney, the back of his players' jerseys had the slogan "Play Hard, Study Harder." The slogan was all about the players and the proper priorities in life. There was no reference to the manager.

That was just the beginning, but it was a blueprint for the entire story. Bugay believed in his players even when his players did not believe in themselves. Every year Bugay found one player that he believed had the ability to bat clean-up (forth) or fifth even if currently he could barely hold a bat. And, if he received a dollar per strike, he would be rich. To that player, Bugay gave tremendous encouragement and the knowledge that he had that position for at least the next five games even if he struck out each time. The same went for a first baseman that could not yet catch all the time, but had the potential to play the position, and so on. By season's end, the players rose to the challenge.

Whenever a parent stood up and shouted at his child, Bugay realized that such behavior put unreasonable pressure on the player and took the fun out of the game. Not so amazingly, as Bugay required the parent to take a step back and let his child enjoy the game, the child thrived emotionally and his performance improved tremendously. Any player that put down another player was told he would bat last, regardless of his talent. Team chemistry was encouraged more than individual accomplishments. It was a team sport and to help build team spirit, Bugay offered pizza and ice cream to the entire team the first time any player hit a legitimate home run.

Coach Bugay, when addressing the players, often associated life's lessons with the game and spoke to the team about important traits such as character, focus, determination, sportsmanship, attitude, and other attributes. Coach Bugay often quoted Los Angeles Lakers coach, Phil Jackson, telling his players that a winner "makes maximum effort, continues to learn and improve and never lets mistakes or fear of mistakes stop [him]." On the lineup card, Bugay often listed famous quotes, for the players to read, designed to get a message across. One of the quotes was from Mickey Mantle, who stated, "After I hit a home run I had a habit of running the bases with my head down. I figured the pitcher already felt bad enough without me showing him up rounding the bases."

Bugay knew that as coach his responsibility was not just to train his players to succeed on the field but, more importantly, he understood that his role was to prepare them to succeed in life. Scott Bugay and Scott Rothstein shared a first name but nothing else. Scott Bugay understood that winning was being a team in which its members respected each other and themselves while, for Scott Rothstein, winning meant having the most toys and cash, and he used everyone in reach to achieve these selfish goals.

Chapter 3

X-rayed on Google

Research is formalized curiosity.
It is poking and prying with a purpose.

~ZORA NEALE HURSTON

AFTER MEETING with Scott Rothstein, I visited the
Clerk of the Court of Broward County's website to see if
there were any lawsuits in which Scott Rothstein or RRA
was either a plaintiff or defendant. There were a handful
of cases, with only a minimal number of dollars involved. For such a
large firm, that did not present a reason for concern.

My attention turned to Google; what I found only confirmed
and amplified what we observed in Rothstein's office. Here was a
man who came from nowhere to completely monopolize the spot-
light. Until founding RRA, Rothstein had been a partner in a small
law firm, living a low-key life. Initially, RRA was comprised of
Rothstein and one partner and five associates, but within seven-and-
a-half years it grew to seventy attorneys. Not surprisingly, Rothstein
was the senior partner.

On November 17, 2008, *SunSentinel.com* columnist Michael
Mayo called Rothstein a *macher*, a "big shot with a persona that's
part Joe Pesci wise guy, part H. Wayne Huizenga entrepreneur, and
part Imelda Marcos spender. Rothstein, forty-six, has roared from

relative obscurity to top of the local power structure in astonishing time."

Mayo pointed out the enormous political contributions Rothstein was making around town, noting that, "Rothstein has become a heavy hitter for the Republican party, contributing hundreds of thousands of dollars this year." He also pointed out that Rothstein was a philanthropist and keenly observed that, while other law firms were not doing as well, both RRA and Rothstein's other business interests were growing. Those interests included real estate, restaurants, and consulting. Mayo wrote, "The Rothstein, Rosenfeldt, Adler Law Firm gets bigger by the month; it's a talented, well-connected collection of former judges, prosecutors, litigators and politicians. When Rothstein founded the firm with Stuart Rosenfeldt in 2002 it had seven lawyers, now it has 62."

Next, Mayo mentioned some of the colorful business associates with whom Scott Rothstein surrounded himself. Scott had partnered with Richard Nixon's former master trickster Republican operative and self-described GOP hit man, Roger Stone. Another infamous association was, "[f]ormer Broward [County] Sheriff Ken Jenne, the disbarred and disgraced Democrat who pleaded guilty to four federal felonies last year." It wasn't a week after leaving federal prison before Ken Jenne was consulting with Rothstein. Mayo ended by stating, "[N]obody knows whether Rothstein's flash will last or whether it's built on quicksand." That observation seemed to be the sentiment of many people once Rothstein entered the scene in his very visible and attention-grabbing way.

Other stories I found helped fill in the blanks about Rothstein and shed light on his curious life. On March 24, 2009, *BrowardBeat.com* columnist Buddy Nevins wrote a piece outlining the generosity of Scott Rothstein and his wife Kimberly. He referred to Scott Rothstein as a "Super Lawyer" and suggested any charity hard hit by recession may want to issue an invitation to Rothstein and his wife. He indicated "[t]he Rothsteins are single-handedly keeping a number of Broward County's charities in the black with their philanthropy."

He mentioned some six-figure and possibly seven-figure donations, yet in his article he never questioned whether Rothstein's persona was real or not. On the contrary, after pointing out, "Scott may be a tad eccentric," he said "[b]ut who cares about Rothstein's idiosyncrasies when he is so generous. Broward is a better place because of Scott and Kimberly."

Comments to this article in March of 2009 on the *BrowardBeat. com* blog were mostly positive, including these:

"[N]evins is right says: … Rothstein is a spur in the side of all law firms. I don't see them contributing to the poor like Scott so they need to shut up."

"[C]ourt gal says Scott Rothstein is a prince. Where is the charity money from Ruden, Greenberg, Schutts, Gunster [other prominent Fort Lauderdale law firms] and the rest of the downtown Fort Lauderdale crowd?"

"Michael G. Alhearn, Esq. says: … I am sure Mr. Rothstein gets asked to participate in many charitable events and from what I have read he is generous to all of them."

However, some who commented on the blog had their suspicions:

"Where is all the money coming from? Who are all these clients? I don't see how all this works and sooner or later that entire thing will have to come to a crashing halt. The law firm is like a levitation trick, you see it but can you really believe it?"

In another article in *BrowardBeat.com* on October 25, 2008, titled "SCHWARZENEGGER COLLECTS BIG MONEY AT ROTHSTEIN PARTY," Buddy Nevins pointed out that Governor Schwarzenegger was able to collect $500,000 "gabbing and shaking hands at the home of lawyer Scott Rothstein." Half of that money came from Rothstein's firm, RRA. These are comments posted by readers to that blog:

"John Bristol says: Knew Scott in law school. Brilliant guy, driven to succeed. Watch out for the haters."

"Ivor Pritchard says: Scott Rothstein put his money where his mouth is – unlike the crusty old Republicans. You go Scotty! Ignore the critics and stand tall for the GOP."

Stand tall he did: on the website *WhitehouseforSale.org*, Scott Rothstein is listed as a bundler for John McCain, having raised at least $500,000 for the Republican candidate.

Other reporters were less impressed. Bob Norman, who works for the *New Times* Broward/Palm Beach office, seemed leery of Scott Rothstein when he wrote the article, "Rise of Ft. Lauderdale attorney has town talking" on Oct. 15, 2008, for the *New Times* blog, *The Daily Pulp*. In that article he commented, "Rothstein's big-spending ways and race to the top of the Fort Lauderdale glitterati has legal and business insiders wondering: Who is this guy? Is he for real, or is he building a house of cards?" Norman also pointed out that Rothstein owned twenty-one cars. They included a Hummer, two Bentleys, three Lamborghinis, a Ferrari, two Harleys, some BMWs, a Mercedes, and some Porsches. And that's not counting the pair of Bugattis he would later buy for 1.6 million dollars each.

Norman wrote that Rothstein was "… snapping up homes, restaurants, commercial real estate, and businesses in South Florida at a breakneck pace." Norman also mentioned the millions Rothstein was distributing among political candidates and his favorite charities. Even his dress was noteworthy of mention. On one particular "casual Friday," Norman commented that Rothstein wasn't "wearing one of his trademark designer Italian suits. Instead he's wearing a designer orange shirt, blue jeans, and orange cowboy boots." Norman also commented on Rothstein's "manic energy that lends to him an air of unpredictability."

Rothstein himself was quoted as saying a couple of interesting things that left me with the same question I had in the beginning: is he always putting on a show and just doing it to generate business, or is he a total fake? In one sentence, Rothstein says, "This is where the evil happens." The next sentence reads, "I tend towards the flashy side, but it's a persona. It's just a f***** persona." All Rothstein did was confirm my concern. He never says which it is: "a persona" or "evil"?

Bob Norman noticed the same thing I did in my first visit. Norman wrote that Rothstein "… comes across as friendly and funny, even gregarious, but he can turn on you in an instant." He described Rothstein as "… something between bravado and bully." Norman wrote: "The flare-up is over as quickly as it started and, soon he's treating me like an old friend, telling me about the stresses of being Scott Rothstein." That is absolutely classic Rothstein. Rothstein says, "[P]eople ask me, 'when do you sleep?' He responds, 'I say I'll sleep when I'm dead. I'm a true Gemini. I joke around that there are 43 people living in my head and you never know what you are going to get."

Great, I thought, *a guy who readily admits to his multiple personalities.*

After Norman wrote about how Rothstein went from "relative anonymity" during the first fifteen years of his law practice to being an equity partner of a major law firm, he then mentions the residential properties Scott purchased. He discusses how in 2003 Scott bought a home for $1,200,000, then a second home on the same street for $2,730,000, then two more homes on the same street, and three homes elsewhere in Broward County, for a total value of $20,000,000.

What I found wasn't just about Rothstein's dubious and amorphous character, but also alluded to an even darker reality. Specifically, I discovered a story in which police from Plantation – a city in Broward County – found the body of Melissa Britt Lewis, an RRA partner, on March 7, 2008, in a canal, and located her car about a mile from her house. The police surmised that she was getting out of her car and going into her home when she was attacked. RRA's chief operating officer's husband, Tony Villegas, was charged with her murder and Assistant State Attorney Howard Scheinberg was the original prosecutor on the case. Many articles published as far away as Iowa questioned whether Tony Villegas committed the murder. There were just too many unusual circumstances that made it look like he was set up. Until April 23, 2010, Villegas was still in jail awaiting trial. He has since been found by the court to be incompetent to stand trial and transferred to a mental health facility. By law, if Tony's mental health does not improve in five years, the first-degree murder case against him must be dropped.

After reading the articles, I didn't know much more about Scott Rothstein than I did after my first meeting, although the murder did raise an eyebrow. Had I known his name, and been able to Google him before going into the first meeting, I probably would have been a lot better prepared for what I saw. Either way, no one seemed to have any idea how he could afford to be as generous as he was and to live as lavishly as he was living. During my next meeting I expected to walk away with that answer.

Rothstein had a 2006 fire-engine-red Ferrari convertible, but with all the vehicles he had, noticeably absent was a 2005 red Ford van, which is the sort of practical vehicle for which Rothstein had no use, but which in my community is used to help others, as witnessed by my next story, "The Red Miracle Van."

The Red Miracle Van

The *Schwartzes* had three vehicles but only two drivers. At any given time the third vehicle, the 2005 red Ford van, could be seen on different driveways throughout the neighborhood and sometimes in Miami Beach, and in Hollywood, Florida.

The Schwartzes kept a third vehicle knowing that not everyone had a car.

Many people come to South Florida because of the excellent

medical care and while they're here they have to deal with the cost of housing and food and the loss of income. The Schwartzes wanted such people to at least be sure they had transportation and didn't have to rely on renting a car or paying for a cab. They first came up with the idea when Rabbi *Rosen* was in town for a liver transplant. The rabbi's family was with him and they didn't have any means of transportation. The Schwartzes realized the Rosen family was saddled with many concerns and although the Schwartzes couldn't solve all of them, transportation was one burden they could remove. For the few months the Rosens were in town, it was the red Ford van they drove.

When other people came to town for medical procedures they drove the red Ford van as well. When a member of the community lost his job and couldn't afford to replace his car, the red Ford van showed up in his driveway. When someone had an accident and the insurance didn't cover a rental, the red Ford van appeared in his driveway. The red van was a lifesaver to so many people. One day, Mr. Schwartz's sister was in town and took the Schwartz children with her to an appointment. An accident occurred and the van was totaled. No one knew how anyone got out of that van alive, but none of the Schwartzes or the driver received so much as a scratch. The Schwartzes' van was a lifesaver for everyone and perhaps that's why it was a lifesaver for them.

It is said that Rothstein gave his law partner, Stuart Rosenfeldt, a red Ferrari as a gift. He also gave his COO, Debra Villegas, a 2009 Maserati GranTurismo. You may think, so then what is so special about the red van? The Schwartzes lent out a vehicle but Rothstein gave away two vehicles.

But in our community the Schwartzes retained the ownership of the red Ford van, paid the insurance, and assumed all of the risk. In our community it was strangers who had the use of the red van more than friends. Our neighbors helped out for the purpose of helping others, not for receiving credit or enhancing their image. Rothstein, it turned out, gave expensive gifts because giving away such luxurious items enhanced his image and helped him gain the confidence that was needed to defraud others. The owners of the red van didn't even want me to use their real names.

Chapter 4

A Third Opinion
Never Hurt

*"Why, sometimes I've believed as many as six
impossible things before breakfast."*

~Lewis Carroll, *Through the Looking Glass*

O N THURSDAY, August 13, 2009, I had an appoint-
ment to meet with my good friend *Moshe Cohen*. We
had planned to meet to discuss a number of different
business opportunities. Moshe was a sharp businessman
and if Rothstein's settlement agreements were real, I knew he'd be
interested in participating. On Tuesday, August 11, I emailed him
around noon and told him that Maurice and I needed to see him for
twenty minutes and it couldn't wait until Thursday. He invited us to
come right over and we did.

Maurice and I sat down to discuss with Moshe our initial meeting
with Scott Rothstein. Moshe was intrigued. I told him it's either
the deal of a lifetime or it's a total fraud. We had reason to believe
it could be either. We asked if he would like to come to the next
meeting because we valued his insight. "The numbers are beyond
phenomenal," we told him. "They are off the charts."

We all quickly calculated how much money we could raise if this was an honest investment. If we found the investment appropriate, and doing business with Scott Rothstein reasonable, we wanted to create a fund and have that fund be Pearson's exclusive investor buying all of Rothstein's clients' settlements. We calculated the tens of millions of dollars a year of profit that would be generated, and we estimated what portion of it would go to the investors and what portion of it would go to us. We began to budget the cost of hiring a securities attorney to prepare a private placement memorandum, and the time it would take to prepare the documents and make other calculations. The idea even came to us that if what Rothstein was doing was so successful, we could speak with employment law attorneys in other major cities who represented plaintiffs. We even envisioned that we could duplicate the system if there was a need and no system in place. Then we stopped dreaming and got back to reality.

We started to write down the questions we were going to ask Scott Rothstein. Again we were going to start with the questions he didn't answer the first time, or the ones whose answers we didn't like. Our agenda quickly became clear: we knew we needed to see the client files and meet the attorneys who handled the disputes. We also would insist on seeing the original settlement agreements. That redacted nonsense, we all agreed, was just that.

Moshe had another great question. He suggested we ask Rothstein for the case attorneys' billing records. Every attorney has a list of hours spent and legal tasks performed during those hours. We didn't care if Rothstein redacted the names but we thought it would be useful if he just showed us the records. We needed to find a basis for establishing the existence of the settlements. We also planned to ask how much malpractice insurance Rothstein carried and if RRA was going to guarantee the investment should the employee speak and the employer obtain an injunction.

Our second meeting with Scott Rothstein was scheduled for later that day. We all agreed we should meet there together and go in as a group. We felt the intoxicating nature of Scott's inner sanctum, as his office was often called, was too dangerous for any of us to be exposed to alone. We felt that if any of us began to be swayed by an illogical argument, the other two could bring the third one back to reality.

Maurice and I drove there together. Moshe was going to meet us, but he was delayed. Our routine now seemed to be that, before going upstairs to meet Scott Rothstein, we would meet Akbar on the ground floor in front of the building. He would bring us up to his office and we would meet with Richard Pearson and then we would go upstairs together. After several minutes of talking that day, Richard stated that Rothstein had to be somewhere and that we really needed to get up to his office because he was leaving and had made a special exception to wait for us.

It seemed like a repeat of the first time. Rothstein was in a rush, but he fit us in and then managed to spend an hour or two with us. Moshe still had not arrived. We decided someone needed to wait for him to bring him up, so Maurice and Akbar went down to meet Moshe and I went into the meeting with Richard Pearson. I did not really like the idea of being there alone. It was too enticing an environment. In a corrupt environment it is important to have someone covering your back and at this point we were not sure if there was corruption, but we knew it was a possibility. As we waited in the corridor to Rothstein's office I saw Rothstein chatting with some ladies in an office just outside his office. Rothstein's conduct was not exactly alarming, but it struck me as inappropriate and it did not conform to the image he had created for himself during our last meeting. There was just something about his behavior that belied his characterization of himself as a champion of ill-treated females.

Just as in the first meeting, my broker came as well. And, just as in the first meeting, David Boden was also present. He was always there, and his presence again seemed to be that of a chief of staff of a high-ranking politician.

At this meeting I noticed something on Rothstein's desk that I did not remember seeing before. It was a beautiful silver canister. Like everything else, it came with a great story and, of course, every story had at its root a large donation that Scott had made. I picked up the silver canister and asked Scott if he knew what it was.

He said, "Yes, it's a beautiful silver canister."

I asked if he knew what was inside and he said, "No." It never even occurred to him anything important was inside. Of course not; appearance was everything.

I said to him that inside the canister was a *megillah*, a parchment with the story of Esther handwritten on it. It is a very significant writing, the original of which dates from the time the Jews were ruled by the kingdom of the Persians. The value of the handwritten document is far greater than that of the container.

My explanation seemed to make no impression on him whatsoever. To Rothstein, it was just a beautiful silver canister. When people saw it, they would have to be impressed by the shiny, expensive silver. End of story.

I spoke with Rothstein for several minutes before Akbar, Moshe, and Maurice arrived. Rothstein mentioned something about how he had been portrayed on a website as running for attorney general. I had seen that site. I brought up some of the comments I read about him in the papers and how he threatened a blog operator to force it to remove a post about him, or else; and it was removed. Scott smiled, clearly because he liked the limelight and even bad news was better than no news for him.

When Akbar, Maurice, and Moshe arrived I thought we would get right back to our questions, but that's not the way Rothstein had it planned. Rothstein must have known that if Moshe came in, sat down, and just asked questions, he would not be as impressed as he would be if he heard the whole story of how powerful a person Rothstein was. So Rothstein walked around his museum of an office with Moshe, showed him the different pictures, and told him the stories that went with each photograph. After we all seemed to be best friends and we were referring to Scott as "Scottie," we sat down to ask questions.

However, before we could begin, Scottie asked David Boden, "Did you tell them about any of our cases?"

David responded, "No."

Scott became very excited; he got up and started walking around and talking to us about some of his cases. His behavior was manic, to say the least.

Scottie started explaining how an employee would come to his office and explain her sexual harassment case. In the particular case Scott described to us, he mentioned that this employee's boss made inappropriate advances toward her, which made Scott really indignant. He put his team to work immediately. They sifted through garbage cans to see what they could find. He suggested that the employee agree to her employer's demands one more time. But this time, Scott would have video equipment placed in the office and everything would be recorded. The employee, of course, agreed and the video was made. Meanwhile in the garbage can, everything was found from the employer's medical records to the Publix supermarket bills, or so we were led to believe.

The next step was for Rothstein to send a letter to the employer, outlining the case and inviting him to bring his attorney to Rothstein's office to see a video of his last performance. Scott was standing at the conference room table and chairs in his office and facing the flat-screen television. He showed us where the employer and his attorney sat and how they faced the television. Scott described how he first mentioned to the employer that he should watch his cholesterol, that, in going through his garbage, he had found a great many empty egg cartons. Then, he pulled out another item that he said he found in the garbage can, to let the employer know that he knew everything about him – or at least about his garbage.

It did not take long to settle this case after the employer saw the video. Scott made it very clear that if the employer wanted to keep his behavior confidential there would be a price. Scott was quite persuasive, but immediately we realized that there could only be so many cases in which all the evidence was videotaped. Perhaps there was one case in a lifetime like that, or maybe one case a year, but could he scale it up in the manner he was talking about? We doubted it. Even if he caught a lot of people with the video, the sound, the garbage, and everything else, a person would need the financial capacity to write an enormous check. Liability without the capacity to pay was meaningless.

Scott kept stressing that so many disputes were being settled because the evidence was so overwhelming that lawsuits never needed to be filed. We wondered whether we were being told that lawsuits were not being filed because Scott understood that our looking in the public records would be a good way for us to verify if the cases really existed, and if so, to identify the other attorneys involved in each case. If they existed, we would also be able to review the court files. When Scott indicated that cases were settled without suits being filed, we needed to know if that was true, since it was more difficult to verify without his assistance, which was not forthcoming.

Scott seemed to recoil upon our requests to see the original settlement documents, meet the attorneys, and meet the clients but, as usual, deflected our questions with another great story. He began to tell us about the prescription pad his crack team found in a doctor's garbage can. Maurice quickly interrupted, asking if it was legal to go through people's garbage.

Scott replied, "Of course it is. That is why it is called garbage. People don't want it so they throw it out, anybody that wants it can have it. It's garbage."

With a smile on his face, Scott continued describing how one of his retired law enforcement officers pulled a prescription pad out of the garbage. There was nothing visible on the pad but it was turned over to a specialist. Scott's team was able to recreate the message from the indentation five pages deep. We got the expletive version, but the substance of what Scott said was on the pad was that one doctor wrote to another that the first doctor was having an intimate relationship with the secretary of the second doctor. He didn't mention if the client came in and found him and hired him or if they went and found the client after they found the prescription pad.

What seemed odd to us was whether this was a sexual harassment case or a hostile work environment case, or perhaps neither one. If the secretary didn't work for the doctor, there was no employer-employee relationship. It may have been a vulgar note, and if the affair really took place it may have been improper or immoral, but was it sexual harassment?

Scott had more stories. As long as we were willing to listen, he was willing to tell stories. He seemed to prefer telling us stories rather than answering our questions, and was happy to offer up some free advice.

"Whenever you throw anything out," he said, "buy a cross-cut paper shredder; one that shreds in both directions. My former law enforcement people, whenever they find shredded documents, they put them all back together. You must shred them in both directions."

We nodded, wondering when he would stop bouncing off the walls.

Either way, the stories just did not resonate with us. What he had represented to us as a typical case was so factually bizarre that the numbers he would later tell us existed had to be fictitious. When listening to Scott, one began to believe that every garbage can was filled with priceless evidence. My vision of Scott's people was of them running around with a garbage truck picking up garbage and sifting through it to create lawsuits. But of course the reality is that most things found in garbage cans are just plain garbage. Unless there is a great case, the amount of time and expense it would take to go through everyone's garbage can is just simply prohibitive and absurd.

From there, Scott jumped into how he built his firm. He said that most firms hire young lawyers and grow the firm that way, but that approach was too slow. Scott hired the best for the head of each practice area and as those lawyers needed help, he allowed them to hire associates. Scott explained that though this was a very expensive hiring practice, it was the reason, he asserted, that his firm had expanded in a sluggish economy while others were contracting. Rothstein even revealed that he had recently acquired a Venezuelan law firm of fifteen or twenty lawyers. We thought that seemed like a strange direction to grow in but we did not ask questions because we were trying to get him back on track. More questions were entertaining but not enlightening.

Already, I feared getting on Scott's bad side. I knew that each time I asked him questions and challenged his answers, I was crossing a dangerous line. All my questions were fair and could easily have been answered if Scott was on the up and up. As a possible investor, I was compelled to do my due diligence at this initial stage. We needed to walk out of his office knowing whether Scott was an entrepreneur or a crook.

Meanwhile, Scott enjoyed the questions from Maurice and Moshe because they were inquiring about becoming his exclusive funder. We thought raising $50,000,000 would be all he needed since money would regularly come back and could be reinvested. We quickly learned that our $50,000,000 would not even plug a small hole in Scott's investment world. Scott did not yet tell us the dollar volume he had available but we were beginning to recognize that it was astronomical, if it existed at all.

Scott sat down for a moment. Just then I realized I needed to start asking questions before he began another story. I asked him how much malpractice insurance his firm had.

He jumped to his feet, "It's irrelevant," he replied, "because if I stole your money, malpractice insurance wouldn't cover me; it only covers negligence."

Good point, we thought, and by now we did have a hunch he was stealing the money. Interesting that he was the one who mentioned it.

Next I asked again about meeting his clients and asked how it could be arranged. Was there a legal way that it could be done?

Again he said, "It can't be done."

"Tell me then," I asked, "who could meet with your client from our side?"

"Only lawyers," he replied.

"I am a lawyer."

He shook his head. "But you don't work for my firm."

I asked him if I could hire a member of his firm, who could then look at the files.

"Absolutely not," Scott said. "You are not to speak with any lawyer in my firm." He was very insistent and made it clear we were to deal only with him.

"*How odd*," I thought. Most CEOs would want us to meet their team but I suppose that would only be if the team was involved with the settlement business.

I asked, "How about the lawyer that handled this case?"

He said, "I handled the case."

I said, "I don't believe you could be handling all these cases yourself. It just doesn't make sense."

He said, "Well, I handle them all. You can talk to me about the case. I handled it."

It wasn't my intention, but Scottie and I seemed to be butting heads a lot during this meeting. At our last meeting I was stonewalled, but this time I intended to leave with some answers. "Scottie," I said, just as I said in the first meeting. "I want to see the file. I need to see the file."

He replied, "Alan, you are making me feel very uncomfortable. You are asking me to engage in criminal conduct and that makes me feel very uncomfortable. I am a member in good standing of the Florida Bar." True enough, at the time.

"Scottie," I said. "I am not asking you to show me your files at random. Your client wants to sell us her settlement. I want to see that file. There is nothing at all wrong with that. There is nothing unusual about that. Even before Bernie Madoff's Ponzi scheme[4] was discovered, it was essential, but post-Madoff, it would be insanity for me not to see that file. So far I have not been given anything to show me that you are dealing with real cases. Everything could have been Photo-shopped and I'm waiting to see something to show me that these settlement agreements are real. I haven't seen anything. If you are not letting me see the file and you are not letting me see the attorney, I'd like you to show me, right now, the billing records for this file. Redact what you like, cross out everything, but show it to me now."

I didn't want him to send the billing records to me the next day. I knew if I agreed that he could send them to me the next day, he would have the opportunity to create fictitious records. As I anticipated, he absolutely refused to even show us the time records.

"Scott," I said, "I am beginning to believe that nothing exists. You are not showing us anything. How can people buy settlement agreements when all they have is a piece of paper with all the pertinent information redacted? It's meaningless. It's foolish."

Scott didn't respond for a minute. He seemed desperate for money, yet he had to realize that we weren't getting anywhere close to asking him for the directions to send him money.

"I have a great idea," he said finally. "I have a young, intelligent, Wall Street-type that is smart as a whip who I want you to meet." Scott explained that one of his big investors convinced him to allow this person to verify the information on the original settlement

---

4 A Ponzi scheme, named after Charles Ponzi, a clerk in Boston who first orchestrated such a scheme in 1919, is a fraud disguised as an investment opportunity. In a Ponzi scheme, initial investors and the perpetrators of the fraud are paid out of funds raised from later investors, and the later investors lose all funds invested. Eventually there isn't enough money to go around and the scheme unravels.

agreement and to see that the wire transfers of funds arrived. We realized that we were not the first people to have these concerns.

"At first," Scott said, "I hated a third-party verifier coming into my office and verifying things, but after a while I saw that the verifier was a nice guy and I actually like him. I never thought I would say this, but I would even be willing to let you meet the verifier and, if you wanted, he could verify your information."

That seemed ridiculous to us. If an independent third party could come in and look at the originals, why couldn't we see them? Scott gave us a lame explanation of how the documents worked and how he was able to have a third party verify it, but it couldn't be us.

"Why?" I asked.

He couldn't give us a good reason, but that didn't matter; by now we were convinced this whole thing was a scam. Yet we also felt like we were in the midst of a ride at Six Flags and, as frightening as it was, it was also exhilarating. By now we had little belief that this was the greatest deal in the world, but we still didn't know if Scott was merely exaggerating and he was only handling a few cases and making it seem like more, or if nothing existed and he was selling a tremendous volume of fabricated settlements.

He reminded us, though, that the settlements we wanted to purchase, each requiring $300,000 a month for three months, were going to be gone soon because he had so many buyers. However, some time had already passed since those settlements were first put out to the marketplace and I thought if they had remained on the shelf this long, something must be really goofy. I reasoned that the employee who had been sexually harassed could have taken the first $300,000 and been out of the financial jam that required her to sell.

True to form, Scott had an answer for my concern. He told us that such employees don't settle until they know there is an investor because the employee wants a cash settlement. It was absurd. What if that employee had to wait thirty or sixty days? She could have had all of her money without the discount and then waited for the last payment. It just did not make any sense. Scott further elaborated that every agreement had a number in it that referred to the settlement number. That was an investor's number.

I have never in my life heard of settling a case only after an investor is found. Most people want to strike while the iron is hot. If an employer is ready to wire money to fund the settlement, why give him time to cool off and change his mind? Nothing made sense in Scott's world. He said we would need to come back within a day or two because these investments would no doubt be sold if we waited any longer.

We explained that Maurice and I had a trade show to attend in Orlando for the International Council of Shopping Centers. Scott said, "They [the settlements] may not be available; we will need to meet before then."

I answered, "It's not possible; we are going to be out of town for a few days."

He said he could wait and he would hold these investments aside for us. *What a guy*, we agreed. *What a guy.*

At the first meeting, Scott had stated that approximately a third of all sexual harassment cases his firm had handled were sold. Before we left our second meeting, I brought up that matter again. It seemed inconceivable that a third of his clients would sell their settlements at such a substantial discount, especially when within thirty days they would be receiving a sizable sum of money regardless of when it was sold.

I told Scott, "I just don't buy it. I just don't believe so many people would sell their settlements." And I asked him also, who determines at what discount they are being sold?

Scott responded, "The client decides the discount rate."

Surprised, I quickly asked, "How come so many $900,000 settlements are being sold for $660,000? It seems odd that they would all pick what they want to sell it for and coincidently it turns out to be the same amount."

Scott admitted that he did give his clients guidance in determining the value of their settlements.

I had noticed that some of the cases were sold for substantially less than others. For instance, the settlements we were considering purchasing were payable over a three month period and were offered to us at a thirty-six percent discount, but there were also settlements payable over ten months at a thirty-three percent discount and some that were payable over eight months at a twenty-seven percent discount. "I don't understand who would buy those," I said.

Scott explained that he had other buyers who weren't looking for big returns. This was a very weak answer, I thought, but I was impressed by how quick on his feet Scott was, like a good trial lawyer. (Mind you, none of the returns were bad and in fact they were all outrageous.) The return an investor would receive from the cases on Scott's list ranged from a low of 67.25 percent to a high of 207 percent. "But all things being equal," we wondered, "why the large spread?"

Scott saw that we were skeptical of his explanation of why so many people would sell their settlements at a substantial discount. At the previous meeting he had explained that it was because the employees were usually behind on their rent but that would only explain a few thousand dollars, not the enormous amounts he was offering.

But at our second meeting, Scott came up with a great new explanation, or at least it sounded like one. He said, "I will tell you why so many clients want to settle. It's because they are qui tam cases." He explained to us about "privity."

In law, "privity" refers to a close, direct, or successive relationship, or to having a mutual interest or right. Scott explained that his clients were in privity with the company they were making the claim against, since they had a sufficiently close relationship to make their claim. Scott said the investors would not be in privity since the relationship was not close enough. He said that if and when a particular qui tam case was taken over by the government, the government could recall a settlement if it had not been fully paid out. But the government can only recall them from a party in privity with the company that settled. The investors are not in privity.

"For the certainty of payment, the clients are willing to accept the deep discount," said Scott.

For once Scott said something that made sense. Of course, we did not know if it was true but, if it was, it would be a logical reason for so many people being willing to take less. Aside from not knowing if it were true, we were concerned that it took Scott so many attempts to come up with a valid-sounding reason. We made a note of this explanation and decided we would contact an employment law attorney to see if there was any truth to it. Scott had also mentioned that the qui tam cases had to be kept confidential. We needed to inquire about that with an employment attorney as well, since employment law was not an area in which any of us had any great in-depth knowledge.

Late into our second meeting we heard a knock at the door. A young lawyer employed by RRA walked in, sheepishly. He seemed to need to muster up the courage to speak to Scottie. He said, "Mr. Rothstein, a couple of us are waiting to see you and have been here for nearly two hours. I just wanted to let you know it's important and we will wait until you are available."

He mentioned the other attorney's name but I didn't catch it. Oddly enough, it appeared as if that attorney was working on real work while Scottie was talking nonsense with us.

Scott, as only Scott could do it, looked over to his "chief of staff," David Boden, and said, "If he ever walks into another meeting of mine, that will be his last day and he will be fired. Please let him know that immediately."

Imagine! Scott was going to be giving out a pink slip to someone for working! We left more certain than ever that we had met a true con man.

After saying goodbye to Rothstein, we went to Pearson's office. Richard liked to debrief us because he needed to see how close he was to earning a commission from us. Pearson was to receive a share of our profits as his commission. We told Richard Pearson we would like to meet people that had already bought settlement agreements through Scott Rothstein. Richard stated that he himself bought around ten-to-twenty million dollars worth of those settlements and he always received timely payments on those investments. We weren't sure if, when he said he bought them, he meant he bought them with his own money or he was just a broker who found the investors and they invested through him. In any event, he assured us that the money came in like clockwork. Moshe asked him if we could see the records, the dates the money was sent and received, the amounts and the settlement agreements. Richard said that he'd be happy to show us everything but, wouldn't you know it? He couldn't find the documents and his bookkeeper was conveniently gone for the day.

After walking out of the second meeting, what came to my mind was the television program that aired in 2004, *My Big Fat Obnoxious Boss*. It was a parody of Donald Trump's TV show *The Apprentice*. Even the boss' name, Mr. N. Paul Todd, was a reference to Donald Trump because the name was an anagram which when unscrambled came out to "Donald Trump." The twelve contestants were all involved in sales, marketing, and the financial market. At the first meeting, Mr. N. Paul Todd described his multi-billion dollar venture capital firm IOCOR. None of the savvy contestants recognized the name, which should have been the first red flag that the show was a spoof since *Iocor* is a Latin verb that means "to jest." The producer just wanted to see how far people would go for a job with the company and a fat salary. Much like Scottie Rothstein, N. Paul Todd started off slowly and ramped things up from the absurd to the totally absurd.

The show was cancelled after five episodes.

If actor William August had not been available to play Mr. N. Paul Todd, Scottie Rothstein would have had the part in a heartbeat and would not have needed a script. If you would ever like to see what Scottie Rothstein was like in action, watch an episode or two of *My Big Fat Obnoxious Boss* on the Internet. It's the closest fictional insight to the sad reality of Scottie Rothstein in person.

Late in the day on August 14, 2009, three days after our second meeting, I retrieved a voice message on my cell phone from Rothstein. I had never given him my cell phone number or my business card so he had to have checked around to get it. This was curious, to say the least, considering how he and I had butted heads. I called him back, and from what he said and his nervous tone, I knew he was desperate for money. He said he wanted to try to see if he could figure out a way to allow me to see at least a little bit of the information that I wanted to see, but in a legal way because, he reiterated, he wanted to keep everything legal. He claimed that there was an exception to the agreement to keep the legal matter confidential: an independent, unrelated party could see the original agreement and proof of the payment as a "confirmer" or "verifier" that it really exists. He thought perhaps I could be appointed to be the "verifier" to look at the name on the original document and also to look on his computer to see that the wire had come in from the accused employer under the settlement agreement. He wanted to make sure that we were going to come back and follow-up, as we said. He said he felt "real comfortable" with me. He repeated this sentiment a couple of times.

How nice, I thought. He likes me, he feels comfortable with me, and he wants to keep everything legal. But if this was so, why was he so inflexible when we met? Was he lying to us then, or was he willing to do something illegal now? There was still a small possibility that he was exaggerating and lying rather than engaged in criminal conduct, but I'd pretty much had it with him. Still, I agreed to the meeting he proposed, though I could not imagine what Scott could possibly show us to change my mind.

The more I thought about honesty and credibility, the more another one of my rabbi's sermons struck a chord. I remember Rabbi Shapiro discussing the difference between falsehood and truth and how even looking at the Hebrew words for "falsehood" and "truth" tells a powerful story. In Hebrew, the word for falsehood is *sheker*. In Hebrew it is spelled שקר. The word for truth is *emes*. In Hebrew it is spelled אמת.

Looking at the letters of שקר *sheker* you can see that none of them can stand on its own. They are not solid. There is no base to them. On the other hand, look at אמת *emes*. All of the letters are solid. Each can stand on its own. Each has a base, a foundation.

This is the Hebrew alphabet in order, from right to left:

אמת

א̄בגדהוזחטיכך‎ל‎מ̄מנן‎סעפ‎ף‎צץקרש‎ת̄

שקר

Sheker שקר contains three of the last four letters in the Hebrew alphabet. You can see them underlined. So if a ruler the length of the Hebrew alphabet was put across all the letters, and the ruler was just placed beginning at the end of the first letter of the word, it wouldn't be able to stand because there would be nothing holding it up on the other end.

Emes, on the other hand, contains the first letter of the alphabet, the middle letter, and the last letter of the alphabet. They are the letters with a line above them. *Emes* can be supported because it has a base. It has a foundation. Each letter of the word can stand on its own. *Emes* is also in order. The first letter represents the first letter of the alphabet, the middle letter represents the middle letter of the alphabet, and the last letter represents the last letter of the alphabet. This is so because truth has to be true, from the beginning to the middle to the end, and it has to be in order. Ninety-nine percent truth is a hundred percent false! Truth in the wrong order is also false. *Sheker*, on the other hand, has the letters mixed up. They are not in order and they are only at the end of the alphabet.

In addition, each letter of the Hebrew alphabet has a numerical value. The numerical value of *sheker* is 600. The numerical value of *emes* is 441. The difference between *sheker* and *emes* is 159 (600 – 441 = 159). The numeric value of *katan* is 159. Interestingly, קטן *katan* means minute or small.

Therefore, there is a small line between *sheker* and *emes*. There is a minute but enormously significant difference between truth and falsehood. And it is tempting, to many people, to cross that small line. Some people even cross that small line unintentionally. But when something cannot stand on its own, we need to question whether it is a mistake and determine if there is an explanation, or whether it is just a falsehood.

In Rothstein's office nothing could stand on its own. All of the pictures and "thank you's" were based on donations. Nothing had a foundation or a base. None of the stories made sense. The documents could not stand on their own because they were all redacted. They were the epitome of what falsehood *sheker* represented. We were still going to meet with Rothstein again, but Rabbi Shapiro's message seemed more and more like a metal detector hitting paydirt.

Scottie's telephone call was completely self-serving. He wanted to be sure I was still on the hook and willing to come back. In my community, there is someone who makes calls for a different reason, and one day I received one of his calls. Enjoy the story "A Welcome Call" and see how a good man spends a few minutes each week to brighten faces.

A Welcome Call

One afternoon before *Shabbos* I received a call from David Barman. I was not surprised to hear from him. We live in the same community. We are both involved in community activities. We are both attorneys and have a lot in common though we attend different *shuls*. The nice surprise was that he was not calling for any other reason than to wish me and my family a good *Shabbos* and see how I was. David told me that every Friday afternoon he makes a point of calling two friends that he does not necessarily run into every week to wish them a good *Shabbos*. He said sometimes it is someone local he hasn't seen for a couple of weeks and sometimes it is someone from out of town who he has not seen for years.

Over the years with a few-minutes investment each week, David has brightened up a lot of lives. He said many people are surprised that he is calling just to say hello and does not have any other purpose in mind. David's sincerity and caring stand on their own – for he makes these calls because he truly cares about people and regrets not having the time to stay in touch. There's no hidden agenda and no return gesture being sought.

This Time it is Check and Checkmate

Whenever you are to do a thing, though it can never be known but to yourself, ask yourself how you would act were all the world looking at you and act accordingly.

~THOMAS JEFFERSON

ON AUGUST 18, 2009, we were scheduled to meet with Scottie Rothstein again. Maurice and I came in one car and Moshe planned to meet us there. As usual, Akbar met us downstairs and we went up to his office on the 12th floor. We spoke for a few minutes with Richard, and then Maurice, Richard, Akbar, and I went to the 16th floor to meet the verifier Scott had said worked for one of the investors. Moshe was going to call us when he was near the office, and Maurice and Akbar were to go downstairs to bring him up.

As we entered, I saw Mike Szafranski, an acquaintance who had an office in the same office building as mine. "Mike," I asked him, "What are you doing here?"

"Alan," he responded, "I am the third-party verifier. What are you doing here?"

"I am the potential investor."

Small town, I thought, *and not in a good way.*

After a few minutes of small talk and looking at the awards on the wall again, we sat down. I took my usual seat on the alligator-skin couch. Scott sat behind his desk and David sat in the seat across from me as he had in the past. This time Miguel wasn't there, but Richard Pearson sat on the far side of the "L"-shaped couch and Maurice and Akbar sat next to him. Mike sat with his back facing away from Scott and me almost as if he were on a witness stand, and in some ways he was.

Scottie started off by praising Mike, describing what a sharp person he was and how efficient he was. It didn't take many questions before I realized that Mike had already "drunk the Kool-Aid." I could see that he believed Scott Rothstein was beyond reproach, as he had objective criteria on which to base this belief. After all, Scott was a member of Governor Charlie Crist's "Kitchen Cabinet" of twenty-five and to be a member of that one had to be vetted. The vetting process is ostensibly a thorough background check.

One would have thought that the extensive verification and examination process Rothstein should have undergone in order to be, as he was then, on the Governor's Council, the Fourth District Court of Appeals nominating committee, and the Broward Sheriff's Advisory Council, would have revealed every questionable activity in which Scott was even remotely involved. Operating a major fraud is not something that could have easily been overlooked if he were properly vetted. One of the brokers in the meeting mentioned that Scott Rothstein had to be the cleanest guy around as he had just gone through the vetting process and had passed with flying colors.

I asked Mike exactly what steps he took to verify the existence of the settlement agreements and the delivery of the wires to the trust account. He explained with confidence that he was the only one permitted to see the original agreements. He explained that he looked at the names of the parties on the original agreement and the amount of the settlement and that Scott Rothstein showed him on the computer that the wire had come in with the same names and accounts on it as on the agreement did.

I asked Mike if he called the bank to confirm that the wire has come in, and he replied, "It wasn't necessary, since Scott already showed me on his computer that the wire came in, and it had the proper amount and the correct reference to the parties."

I asked him if he ever saw the actual file and he replied that he did not.

"I was told that the file was confidential," he explained to us.

"How about speaking with the attorneys involved?" I asked.

Quickly Scott jumped to his feet and said, "I am the attorney on all of the cases."

I said, "It doesn't seem possible."

I still couldn't believe he could handle all those cases himself and I again stated to him that I believed it was impossible for him to do so. "I want to speak to the attorney who worked on them."

"I am the attorney who handled the cases," Scott again said.

"Mike," I said, turning to the verifier, "how many cases have you verified and have confirmed the arrival of the corresponding wires?"

"750," Mike responded.

"750!" I responded, quite surprised.

"Yes."

What I thought would be my final question for Mike was, "What's the lowest amount you saw a settlement for?"

Again, I was dumbfounded when Mike replied, "$500,000."

"Let's figure this out," I said. "You verified 750 cases in how long a period of time?"

"Eighteen months."

"Okay," I said. "That's about 500 cases a year, correct?"

"Yes."

"And you handle the verification for about half of the cases. Is that correct?"

"Yes."

Then that means the firm sells about 1,000 cases a year."

"Correct."

I mentioned that Scott had told us that about a third of the cases were sold, and his clients take payments on the other two-thirds.

Scott interrupted and said, "Yes."

At this point, if we were playing chess, Scott's position would have been the equivalent of check.

I pointed out to Scott that if 1,000 cases were being verified as their wires come in for sales, his firm must handle 3,000 cases in a year. At that point Scottie knew his whole argument was illogical. He tried back-pedaling by explaining that "a lot of the cases had multiple plaintiffs so that while there are a lot of settlements, many of them relate to one case."

I asked Mike if that was correct.

Mike replied, "Most of the wires I verified were individual cases." At that point, it seemed that, even though he had drunk the Rothstein Kool-Aid, he wasn't about to lie to me about what he observed.

I had figured out that even based on the very, very low end of a settlement of $500,000 per case, if there were indeed 3,000 cases, then Scott was pulling in a *billion*-and-a-half dollars a year. This did not take into account Scott's statement that many of the cases had settled for millions of dollars. Since legal fees were traditionally a third of that amount, Scottie's take was a half-billion dollars in fees for the cases that he handled himself. And again, that's on the low end since many of the cases were in the millions of dollars.

Even in a 250-day work year, each day, Scottie would have to settle twelve old cases and bring in twelve new cases and then find some time to work on these cases. He also would need time to speak with his pool of investors. It was absolutely impossible. At the time I was told his firm had ninety-three lawyers. I quickly divided a half-a-billion dollars by 100 lawyers and thought to myself, *If Scott is personally earning $5,000,000 per lawyer in his firm, why would anyone work on anything else?* Yet I knew not all of the attorneys were involved with these cases. *This whole thing*, I thought, *is becoming truly ridiculous.*

I asked Mike how the return could be over 100 percent a year when the risk was so minimal. He said he was told it was due to the lack of transparency. Apparently a lot of people did not like investing when the document they received was completely redacted. For Mike's investors this didn't seem to make a difference since Mike was able to see the original settlement agreement. I mentioned that based on the way the entire process took place, it could be that Scottie doctored all of the wires that came in and therefore the verification Mike made was useless. I asked Mike how he knew that the original settlements were real and that they weren't just doctored along with the wires.

Mike was offended. From the expression on his face it was obvious that he really believed in Scott Rothstein. Perhaps all of the testimonies on the walls, the awards, the pictures, the letters from charitable organizations, sports stars, politicians, and law enforcement personnel were believable to him. After all, the entire purpose of decorating the room with awards was to create that impression, and to an impressionable person, Scott was the man. Sprinkle in the idea that a person could make hundreds of thousands of dollars, perhaps millions of dollars by purchasing, verifying, and brokering settlements, and soon everything looked real. Being in Scottie's office was almost like being in Disney World with 3-D glasses. Everything looked real and within reach, but as soon as you reached out, nothing was there.

Then Mike said that if I didn't like the lack of transparency and if I wasn't comfortable with the lack of transparency, perhaps I was not the right kind of investor for these settlements.

Scottie added, "I don't think you understand how this business works."

"I think I understand too much how it works," I snapped back. "That's the problem."

It was beyond belief to see someone trying to scam us and, simultaneously, to witness other people in the room so gullible and oblivious as to believe the unbelievable. Maurice was totally intrigued by what was again like a roller coaster ride, but I had had enough, and knew this had to be my last meeting.

Scott seemed quite fed up with me. He couldn't change the numbers that he had already provided to us, even though now it was obvious that these numbers had to be fictitious. After Scott told me that a third of his cases were sold, and Mike told me how many he verified and what the lowest amount was, it was all simple arithmetic, which obviously no one else had taken the time to do. I mentioned that post-Madoff, it was impossible for anyone to say, "Just believe in me," and for the investor not to demand to see concrete evidence of the proposed investments. Everything I had seen could have easily been explained by doctored documents.

The brokers weren't sure whether we were going to buy or not buy. Scott understood I wasn't buying anything but he still may have thought that Maurice believed in him because Maurice was non-confrontational. I knew that many other people were buying. I guess that gave Scott good reason to believe absolutely anybody is a potential sucker, as long as he flashed enough money and made the dream look real enough.

The verification method was apparently acceptable for Mike's investors, who presumed that Scott was honest and his integrity was beyond reproach. All that Mike's client seemed to require was mere verification that the wire from the employer involved in the settlement of a possible lawsuit came in and that there were no mistakes. He assumed that Scott would not be involved in fraudulent conduct. But we were looking for real due diligence, not a mere verification that names on agreements and wires matched. We needed to see the actual settlement agreements and to meet with the attorneys from Scott's firm who were handling the cases.

Imagine you are meeting with a person whose reputation you feel is beyond reproach. How could you have the nerve to ask such a person to verify what he says? It's difficult, but when you invest your own money or, even more so, someone else's money, every reasonable question needs to be asked. This is the due diligence that every investor relies upon before agreeing to an investment, and it is the only way to reduce the risks of bad investments and to have half a chance of exposing fraud. Performing a thorough due diligence will not solve every problem, but it will eliminate a lot of bad deals and expose a lot of as yet unidentified risks.

But looking at Scott Rothstein, I didn't believe his reputation was beyond reproach. At the beginning, of course, I did believe he was a legitimate attorney, albeit quite eccentric, and I quickly understood that he wasn't very willing or appreciative of being asked to verify what he was saying. However, having a great reputation is not a free pass that exempts a person from having to prove who he is, or what he is all about, and what he is selling and what he is delivering. When studying the ancient prophets, I learned this lesson.

At the time of the prophets, there was no shortage of people stepping up and claiming that G-d talked to them, but for a prophet to be considered a true prophet in Judaism, the prophet was obligated to prove himself. Proof didn't come in the form of making donations to all the leaders and receiving a letter saying how amazing the person was. It didn't come from making contributions to all the needy causes and receiving a letter of greatness. It didn't come from rubbing elbows with the most affluent people and receiving their endorsement. Proof of a prophet came from the prophet stating with specificity a miracle that would take place, and then that miracle would have to take place absolutely to the letter of the prophecy. For example, if a prophet said that in three days an apple tree on a certain parcel of land would have 200 apples, 100 red apples, and 100 green apples – and three days later, a large apple tree had 200 apples, 150 red apples, and fifty green apples, the prophet was considered a false prophet. To prove prophecy, even the number and color of the apples had to be true.

So how could I sit in front of Scott Rothstein and give him a free pass on verifying anything? We didn't give free passes to our prophets and we certainly can't give free passes to modern-day promoters. If a person has something worth selling, he should be only too pleased to verify what he claims. Thousands of years after the prophets, people are still following profits but unfortunately today our profits are with an "f" and not with a "ph"!

After the meeting, we walked outside. I knew that I had to talk to Mike alone, without Scottie, to see if he was for real. Mike seemed to absolutely, positively believe that Scott was an upstanding member of the community and one of the most highly regarded attorneys in Broward County. In a way, Mike's impression of Scott's was correct; Scott was highly regarded. Mike also seemed to believe that the documents he saw were in fact original settlement agreements. I felt at least my questions should have created a slight bit of doubt, and perhaps they did, but he gave no indication of it. Mike was more than twenty years younger than me and couldn't imagine a prominent lawyer lying and stealing.

I wanted to believe the same, but as hard as I tried, and I did try hard, Scott did not give me a valid reason to believe him. I was not about to accept the stamps of approval written all over his walls since they were all bought, and originally, I thought bought with his own money. Now, I was beginning to think they were bought with investors' money. I am a big believer in people and I always will be, but Scott did not earn my belief in him. There were too many red flags. None of the numbers or the activities were within the range of customary activities or even close to realistic.

How could it be that after our meeting with Mike Szafranski that Mike and David Boden and the brokers did not realize Rothstein was a scammer even if before the meeting they did not know it? How could it not have at least created a doubt in their minds? In fact, why did so many people ignore the signs and invest with or become involved with Rothstein? Consider the following from the Torah regarding the plagues in Egypt:

The first six plagues against Egypt came true just as Moses had told the pharaoh they would. There was nothing the Egyptians could do to avoid them short of freeing the Jews. Not so, however, with the seventh plague, the plague of hail. That plague was essentially a voluntary plague. Moses urged the pharaoh to have the people and animals brought inside so that they would not be killed by the hail. Moses told them that all the men and animals left outside would be killed the next day.

The Egyptians had two ways to avoid being harmed by the hail. Either they could repent or they could stay inside and bring their animals inside as well. The first six plagues could not have been easily avoided, but the hail could have been. Yet most Egyptians ignored the opportunity to save their animals and even many people stayed outside. The question begs to be answered. The Egyptians had already witnessed the first six plagues coming about just as Moses warned. With Moses having a six-for-six record, the people must have believed that the seventh plague would occur just as Moses said. So if it was a voluntary plague, why would most people not bring their animals inside?

Our neighbor, rabbi and author Avraham Yachnes, shared with us at a *Shabbos* lunch how Rabbi Yaakov Yisrael Kanievsky, the Torah scholar known as The Steipler, who passed away in 1985, answered the question by explaining a facet of human nature.

The Steipler said that once a person makes up his mind, he will not allow the facts to change his decision. A person will simply ignore any facts that disprove or draw into question his decision. This may well explain how so many warning signs that should have prevented a prudent investor from investing with Rothstein were ignored. Once people saw the pot of gold they would receive from Rothstein, they were not about to let the facts interfere with their decision. This answer may also explain how others who were benefiting from his conduct also kept their eyes closed to the warning signs. We could see from this how important it is to seek advice from an objective, disinterested person when we need to make important decisions.

That day, after our meeting, Maurice called Moshe and told him we had finished so he might as well turn around and head back. Moshe said he was only about five minutes away and wanted to stop in and say hello to Scottie, so we waited for him. When he arrived, we all went back up with Moshe to say a quick hello. Scott was glad to see Moshe. One thing about Scott was that he never gave up trying to get money from people. He knew that "No" only meant, "Not yet."

On the ride home after the third meeting, Maurice said that he'd like to go back to Scott's office. I said that I didn't think I could set foot in there again. I didn't think I would be welcome. Maurice agreed it was a Ponzi scheme, but he just wanted to visit one more time. Never had he seen such a show.

I told Maurice that absolutely positively this was a Ponzi scheme and there was no possible way to explain Scott's conduct otherwise. Over the next two or three weeks, Maurice, Moshe, and I met for lunch or coffee a few times and on a couple of occasions just Moshe and I met. We continued to want to believe that Scott was not a scammer. We wanted to find the good in him. We were hoping to discover he was just a salesman embellishing the numbers. We tried everything to prove that this was not a Ponzi scheme, but just couldn't do it.

By the beginning of September 2009, Moshe had spoken with his attorney to find out the answers to our questions on the qui tam cases: first, if the government took over a qui tam case, was there a risk that settlements that were not fully paid out could be rescinded? Second, did there need to be privity between the parties? And third, was it important to keep the whistleblower cases quiet? Moshe learned that Scott had given us misinformation on all counts. First, Moshe was told that partially settled payments are not at risk of being cancelled by the government. Second, selling the settlement to an unrelated party does not affect a settlement being honored. Third, the company would want the public to be aware of the whistleblower action. That prevented other people from stepping up and also filing a whistleblower action. It seemed like there was no other explanation. Ponzi was the name of the game.

Moshe had to be out of town for the next week but we met again when he returned to Miami. Unbelievably, Moshe told me that while he was in New York he was approached by a friend to see if he wanted to participate in a great investment that involved a prominent Broward County law firm that was selling a few settlement agreements involving its clients. He was told that these settlements were only being sold to a few select people. This was an approach Scottie borrowed from Madoff. Let people believe that only certain investors were being asked to invest in your product.

Moshe indicated that he was not interested and that he suspected the whole thing was a scam. Moshe's friend wanted to know how he knew, and Moshe explained how he had met with Scottie. Moshe's friend then asked Moshe to meet with another individual he knew who was planning to invest $35,000,000 in the "settlement agreements." Moshe hated to see anyone lose his money so he spent two hours in the middle of the night posing questions, revealing the red flags so the person would not invest his group's money. To his surprise, this person not only invested the money but perhaps invested much more. No one wanted to believe that these settlement agreements were not real.

One interesting development Moshe noticed was that since these out-of-town investors were now somewhat concerned, they asked for more security. Scottie was so glad to see $35,000,000 coming his way that he apparently set up a bank account with TD Bank in the amount of $50,000,000 irrevocably in the names of those investors. Scott led them to believe that $50,000,000 was from the employer that was settling the matter. By making the account irrevocable, it meant the designated recipient of the funds in the account could not be changed. That seemed illogical and it threw us for a loop. What happened if the $35,000,000 these investors had been promised were never deposited? How Scott would get back his $50,000,000, we had no idea. We were told that these investors had confirmed with the bank that the $50,000,000 account existed in their names, and that the account was irrevocable. Now we were dumbfounded. Moshe said it couldn't be a Ponzi scheme because, if it were such a scheme, how could he take the $50,000,000 out before the money came in? And how could Scott benefit by putting aside $15,000,000 more than he had coming in?

Moshe said this must somehow be a money laundering scheme. He said, "Don't you get it? Look at all the businesses Scottie recently bought into, all those Bova restaurants, the Versace Mansion, the watch business, and the vodka business, to name just a few. They are all businesses that he could be cleaning his money through." With Burger Kings, the revenue department could easily determine how many hamburgers were sold a day and calculate the likely revenue and expenses. But with high-end restaurants and the Versace Mansion, millions of dollars could be funneled through there, and the revenue department would not easily know that the amount of revenue being generated was suspect, since each of those places was so unique. It all seemed to make sense.

We also knew from Scott that RRA had just purchased a law firm in Venezuela with fifteen-to-twenty lawyers. Maybe money would be funneled through that law firm to launder the money. Perhaps it was drugs or gun-running. We thought maybe the money needed to get to Venezuela. Even though the Ponzi scheme may have cost Scott a third or half of his profits, it generated large amounts of "clean" money that could then be sent to Venezuela if that was where it needed to go. Contracts could have been drawn and documents prepared to make it look like investments were being made in Venezuela. The money could have been sent to the Venezuelan law firm and distributed to the drug lords or gun-runners there, if that was its destination.

Moshe did not like the Ponzi theory, since a person would have to be stupid to pay such high returns and to pay them so soon. He gave Scott more credit than to create a scheme that would by its very nature collapse early on in the process. Now if money was coming in from another source like drugs or guns, then it would not disintegrate as long as profits from the drugs or guns were flowing.

Moshe and I went up and back during the next two meetings with theories. I still believed it was a Ponzi scheme. It just had Ponzi written all over everything we saw. It could have been Ponzi and money laundering, I thought, but it was Ponzi at least in part. I mentioned to Moshe we were trying our best to find a way to confirm that the transactions were legal and that Scottie was an honest person so we did not have to report him to the government.

But I said, "Don't you see? The more we keep discussing it, the more we just come up with more illegal theories. No one is proposing that there is even a possibility that Scottie is engaged in legal activities."

His lifestyle with the expensive houses, cars, boats, donations and travel on private planes had to cost at least ten-to-thirty million dollars a year and maybe many times more than that. I thought to myself, *There is nothing more to talk about with respect to Scottie's business being legal.* Now we just had to figure out what we could do to prevent other people from being scammed by Scottie, since we did not want other people to be harmed.

Scott liked to tell stories about employers that took advantage of employees, but he was the one taking advantage. Unlike Scott's stories, this one, that I call "A Piece of His Mind!" is about one person truly looking after the interests of another.

A Piece of His Mind!

Arlene Canner was a hard worker and excellent secretary. She was quick and efficient even before there were computers in the office. Working for a group of orthopedic surgeons kept her very busy. When Arlene's boss, Dr. Joel Dennis, became president of the Samuel Scheck Hillel Community Day School, the new day school he helped, with others, to found in North Dade County, Florida, the responsibilities of keeping the office running and also handling work for the school doubled her workload. Arlene mentioned this to her husband, Irv, who said he would drop in and give Dr. Dennis a piece of his mind. Irv did drop in, but after hearing about the quality of education and type of curriculum Hillel was offering for its students, instead of giving Dr. Dennis a piece of his mind, Irv gave him a helping hand. Arlene stayed on the job for twenty years and Irv and Arlene joined the group that became the founders of Hillel. Over the next thirty years, Irv became the executive vice president and was a member of the Executive Committee, and he and Arlene served on the Board of Directors.

Over time, tuition became costly and beyond the reach of many. Irv Canner created for himself a new challenge – he wanted to ensure that every student who attended, or wished to attend Hillel, but who could not afford full tuition, received a scholarship for the portion beyond his family's means. Irv would pick up the phone and call or even visit everyone he could to raise the funds necessary to cover the scholarships. Often times, part of the funds came from Irv Canner's own pocket. With the help of Irv and his fellow founders and board members, Hillel grew to 1,500 students with a $15,000,000 budget.

Irv Canner's acts of kindness are acts that Scott Rothstein apparently could never comprehend. Rothstein only knew how to take funds from other people – often times, a person's life savings – to fuel his unconscionable greed.

Chapter 6

The Red Flags

*The sun shines and warms and lights us and
we have no curiosity to know why this is so;
but we ask the reason of all evil, of pain, and
hunger, and mosquitoes and silly people.*

~RALPH WALDO EMERSON

F OR ME, at this point, the die was cast, and my decision
was clear. I could not be involved with what by all objective
measurements was a textbook Ponzi scheme, engineered
masterfully by Rothstein and fueled by his charm. Twelve
major red flags presented themselves:

1. The list of investments Akbar had given us to consider showed
eighteen settlement agreements. Nine were crossed through
because they had already been sold. Oddly, the best ones were
left and some of the worst ones were sold. (Was I to believe I was
smarter than most of the other investors?)

2. The returns exceeded 100 percent per annum. Several were over
200 percent per annum with minimal risk. Factoring, which is
basically what this was, with such low risk, should have yielded
fifteen-to-twenty percent per annum returns. Factoring is in
essence advancing cash on the basis of accounts receivable. That
is when a person, a factor, advances to the person who expects to

receive money a percentage of the money that will soon be due. When the money is paid, it will belong to the factor.

3. Scottie personally settled over 3,000 disputes per year without filing any lawsuits. This was an implausible number since a very productive firm, focusing solely on employment law, would most likely just handle a small fraction of that number. Such a firm would probably, even in a great year, only settle a handful of cases for $500,000 or more without a lawsuit.

4. The minimum settlement was for $500,000. This number, coupled with the number of claims, was preposterous. It meant that if the disputes were settling for Scottie's lowest amounts, Scottie was personally settling over 1.5 billion dollars in disputes per year without a single lawsuit ever being filed in court. That number was actually conservative since many of his fabricated settlements were in the several million dollar range. His legal fee was one third of the first million dollars. So on the low end, his legal fees were a cool half-billion dollars. It did not make any sense, especially since Scott said he was the only attorney that worked on those cases. It defied logic. Even if such a large number of cases was real and Scott had evidence that was sufficiently damning to merit such settlements, the accused individuals and companies would have still needed the financial capacity to make such payments. Regardless, even if all of this existed the way that Scott had described it, Scott would have averaged $250,000 an hour and that is assuming the cases settled for the low amounts, not the several million dollars as Scott described. Not likely, to say the least.

5. One third of Scott's clients were willing to sell their settlements at a substantial discount. If investors were to earn 200 percent and more on their investment, in essence, it would be the investor that would receive that return out of the settlement that would otherwise go to the clients. With the money in RRA's trust account and large disbursements being paid within only thirty days, why would any plaintiff (the party bringing suit) do it? It is just too

much to give away for what amounts to a thirty-day loan. And whoever heard of settling 3,000 cases a year with monthly payouts, but with none of the settlements including even a portion of the settlement being paid at the time of signing the settlement? It just could not be that a third of Scott's clients would sell settlements at such ridiculously inflated terms.

6. Scott's excuse for keeping the sales of settlement agreements confidential was weak. He said he feared that the other attorneys would discover that the settlement agreements did not prohibit assignability. If that happened, this niche market Scottie created would disappear. It was inconceivable that if there were truly 3,000 matters being settled annually, not one opposing attorney realized the payments were assignable. Our community has highly talented attorneys and drafting a contract that cannot be assigned is basic for even a first-year attorney. There is no way that so many experienced attorneys, one after the next, would miss such an obvious omission in a settlement agreement.

7. Richard Pearson and Scott Rothstein indicated that a hedge fund had been a significant funder of the settlement agreements but due to financial difficulty, it was not going to be funding any new investments. That raised an eyebrow since if the hedge fund was in need of higher earnings, what could be better than 100-to-200 percent returns with minimal risk? Did the hedge fund operators discover something illegal about the settlement agreements they were purchasing?

8. Scottie's business plan that we received before meeting with him the first time implied that many of the cases were coming from Internet sites and campaigns with 1-800 numbers. If he was generating substantial business from Internet sites, I should have been able to locate at least one of them. When I searched, I could not find any.

9. I was not permitted to conduct basic due diligence – to meet the client selling the settlement, to see the client's file, to speak with the RRA attorney assigned to the case, or to see the original

settlement. All Scottie was willing to give me was a redacted copy of the settlement agreement. When asked to immediately show me the attorney's time records, even with redacting the names so I would know a real attorney spent real time on this case, Scottie refused. I am sure if I gave him a couple days to create one, he would have done so, and it would have been complete fiction.

10. The investor was not required to invest until the investor's unique identification code was put on page two of each settlement agreement being purchased and then the settlement proceeds required by the settlement agreement were received into RRA's trust account. This was a Catch-22. How could the investor's code be in the settlement agreement before the prospective investor made the required investment? What would happen if the investor failed to proceed with an investment and the agreement was already executed with the investor's code in it? This illogical and unlikely system became even more suspicious to us once we were told that in a recent transaction there was an irrevocable agreement with the bank that the account was to be paid to a particular investor. We did not understand why Scott would take such a chance before receiving the investor's money – unless of course everything was fabricated and/or he was laundering money.

11. Rothstein's lifestyle was inconsistent with his position. Scott was living as if he was earning tens of millions of dollars a year but there was no indication that his firm was generating the kind of money he was spending. Most lawyers, even heads of firms, are not earning tens of millions a year; certainly not employment law firms. Even if Scott had won a lottery, it would not have been an adequate explanation since he was spending more than the average lottery paid out. Scott leased a jet, bought a $5,000,000 Warren yacht, and owned a fleet of one of almost two dozen exotic cars including a Bentley, a Rolls-Royce, two Lamborghinis, two Ferraris, and two Bugatti sports cars worth 1.6 million dollars each. He bought a mansion and then bought the other houses on the same street. He invested in business after business.

12. The suspicious death of Melissa Britt Lewis constituted the final red flag. Melissa, a partner at RRA, was murdered in March of 2008. There were too many unusual circumstances surrounding the case, especially when it is possible that she had learned that a Ponzi scheme was in full operation at her firm. She may have tried to stop what Rothstein was doing, at the cost of her own life.

The original theory of Lewis' demise was simple: she was followed home from Publix supermarket and robbed, and then murdered by the perpetrator, who disposed of her body in a canal. But evidence pointed to the involvement of Tony Villegas, estranged husband of Debra Villegas, who was the chief operating officer of the RRA law firm.

There were three pieces of strong evidence pointing to Tony, perhaps even four: the police and prosecutors say Tony Villegas' DNA was found on Melissa's body; Melissa's cell phone was tied to signals reaching out to towers along the route Tony Villegas lived and along the train route he worked; Tony's computer was said to have a Google search for a way to get rid of pepper spray; and his roommate said that he was observed washing pepper spray from his body and clothes.

But, just perhaps, Melissa knew what Scott Rothstein was up to and she was not about to stand idly by and let the public be harmed by this scam artist. The newspapers reported that she was best friends with Debra Villegas. They were both going through ugly divorces at the time. Melissa had completed her divorce; Debra had not. If Debra and Melissa were very, very close friends, is it possible that Debra may have told Melissa what was going on with Rothstein's Ponzi scheme? Or could Melissa have guessed and told Debra of her suspicions? Could it be that someone thought this might be a good way to kill two birds with one stone? Debra's contribution to the firm was certainly valued. I did not know this then, but later it was revealed that she was the absolute second in command person in the firm and her work was invaluable to Scott and the Ponzi scheme.

She was also being represented in the divorce case by Scott Rothstein himself. Debra Villegas and Scott Rothstein had access to thugs and law enforcement. They could have easily framed Tony Villegas if they felt he was in their way. Interestingly, Tony Villegas did not have a prior criminal record.

After Melissa's death, a $20,000 donation to endow a Broward College scholarship in her memory was made by RRA. It sounds nice, even generous. But was it, or was Rothstein asked by name to make a donation and embarrassed not to? Twenty thousand dollars is a lot of money but Rothstein routinely gave out $50,000 for almost any cause and on a number of occasions gave $1,000,000. Remember, he could be a sport, but always with stolen money. I did not know it at the time, but Scott paid $100,000 to a Don Henley environmental cause in exchange for the band leader to dedicate *Life in the Fast Lane* at an Eagles concert in January 2009, to Scott and his wife Kimmie for their first anniversary. Twenty thousand dollars was just chump change for him. If he really cared about Melissa and truly wanted to honor her memory, it would seem he would give at least $50,000, or more, to charities connected with her name.

Later on, these facts came out: In July of 2009, Scott deeded a house he owned in Weston, Florida, having a tax assessed value of $475,000, to Debra Villegas for $100 and "love and affection." Essentially it was a gift. Rothstein also gave Debra a 2009 Maserati GranTurismo. Her salary was $250,000 per year and she advanced from the position of paralegal to the COO of RRA, all without a college degree.

What about the evidence? The DNA? Maybe something with Tony's DNA was planted, maybe it wasn't. Maybe it was fabricated. On August 17, 2009, the *New York Times*, in an article written by Andrew Pollack, reported that, "Scientists in Israel have demonstrated that it is possible to fabricate DNA evidence, undermining the credibility of what has been considered the gold standard of proof in criminal cases."

How about the cell phone that was tracked right near Tony

Villegas' home and along the route he worked? If he was framed, certainly it was easy for the person who wanted him framed to have someone take the telephone along that route and then get authorities to track the phone and see if it led to any clues. The same with the pepper spray. Is it possible that somebody called the defendant and asked him if he could look up on his computer how to get rid of pepper spray? If someone had asked Tony, it would be just as visible on his computer as if he did it for his own reasons.

In addition, Tony Villegas' attorneys have cited the following facts in Tony's favor. First, thirty-nine-year-old Melissa Britt Lewis spent her last day alive asking two law firm colleagues about preparing a will. Also, according to former RRA attorney Carl Linder, Melissa said that she had been under a lot of stress and had actually gone for a cardiac stress test in the weeks before her murder. Further, in an early interview with police, Debra Villegas said she was "99.9 percent sure" that Tony had had nothing to do with Melissa's death. She changed her position in later interviews. Also, in his first interview with the police, Tony's roommate Wilset Pascual didn't mention anything about pepper spray, a computer search, or Villegas scratching himself when Pascual saw him the night of the murder. His story changed after the *SunSentinel.com* article about pepper spray appeared. However, the computer records do confirm the existence of a search on pepper spray. And lastly, former RRA attorney Christina Kitterman told police that Melissa confided a great deal in RRA co-founder Stuart Rosenfeldt. She said that if Melissa was afraid of someone, she might have talked to Stuart Rosenfeldt about it. The police did not formally interview Mr. Rosenfeldt.

On the other hand, the police investigation paints Tony Villegas as a controlling husband and physically abusive father. Debra Villegas told the police that she lived in fear of what he would do if she ever left him, and she had only gotten up the courage to leave him because he was becoming increasingly abusive to the children. According to court documents, the Villegas children backed her account. Their teenage son told police that his father repeatedly blamed Melissa for

Debra's break-up with him. Further, a day planner seized from Tony Villegas' home indicated that he had had difficulty getting over the end of his marriage. Police said he wrote such passages as, "She don't love you. She laffing [sic] at you," and "She look like she in love."

Further, a nurse at the medical office building where Melissa's SUV was abandoned identified Villegas' silver Corvette as being in the parking lot that night. It was known that Tony Villegas drove a silver Corvette.

However, it is not clear why the nurse would have thought the car belonged to Tony. Silver is a popular car color and there are a lot of Corvettes in Florida. And even if it really was Tony's car, and if he were being framed, it would not have been too difficult to plant the car or a similar car in that parking lot. It is certainly possible that Debra had a set of keys to it, or got a key made by the dealership. At that point she was still married to Tony Villegas.

According to *The New Times'* investigative reporter, Bob Norman, in an article in *The Daily Pulp* on December 3, 2009, "… Scott Rothstein held a position of special influence with both the Plantation Police Department and the initial prosecutor, Howard Scheinberg, who subsequently left the State Attorney's Office to work for Rothstein."

Scott's head of security was a former Plantation police officer. Rothstein was also the attorney for the Plantation police union. Scheinberg could have received an offer he could not refuse to join RRA with no sinister intent. But why would Scott hire the prosecutor if Scott did not think he needed to reward him or get him off the case? Rothstein really had a knack for blurring all the lines. Even if Tony Villegas did commit the murder, all of the oddities in the case created a lack of confidence in the system.

All this mystery related to Scott Rothstein and his greed machine.

Perhaps there was even an additional red flag had I thought about it more: the Scroll of Esther on Scott's desk. It seemed odd, and out of place, but maybe it wasn't. Maybe it was a signal of what was really going on behind the scenes. In Hebrew, the Scroll of Esther is called *Megillas* Esther. It is read on the Jewish holiday of *Purim*. Once before *Purim*, Rabbi Shapiro pointed out that the derivation, of the word Esther, as in *Megillas* Esther, is *hester*, meaning hidden. However, the word *hester* has two additional meanings as well, contradiction and destruction. Rabbi Shapiro points out that these three meanings for *hester* are directly related to one another because what is hidden often leads to contradictions which frequently result in "destruction." The root of the word *Megillah* (singular of *Megillas*) means "reveal." It is amazing that the definition of the roots of both words was an early warning system, letting everyone know they would need to reveal what was hidden and identify the contradictions in order to stop the destruction.

At this point, I realized that I needed to do everything I could to stop Scott Rothstein from harming other people. He was a danger to society. He was also a control freak who, like a mobster, had connections to law enforcement and politicians. Stopping him wasn't as simple as just turning him in. To whom could he be turned in? He knew so many people in the right places – or, as Garth Brooks might have put it, he had low friends in high places – and so much money flowed to them, that if it appeared that an investigation into allegations he was engaged in criminal activities was being conducted, someone who knew him would be quite surprised because he was Mr. Broward County.

Without even having bad intentions, someone might tip him off that an investigation was being conducted. At that point, his well-oiled machine, gobbling up tens of millions of dollars at a time, would not have been able to be stopped by one person or one investigation. To say that "money blurs vision" would be an understatement, and getting in the way of Scott spreading all of that money around created a clear danger. I understood that I better be concerned if Rothstein found out I reported him to authorities for masterminding and engaging in a colossal Ponzi scheme, while hiding behind a legitimate law firm.

I often wondered how his scheme could have continued for four-and-a-half years without somebody else having already turned him in. If he had been unmasked a long time ago, by this time the operation would have stopped. Perhaps others had exposed him days or weeks or maybe a few months before me, but, I thought, the investigation must not be completed if Scottie was still operating so brazenly openly.

Relying on the possibility that someone else might have blown his cover was no excuse for inaction on my part because, if it wasn't true, Scott could continue to harm other people. Now was the difficult part. I needed to find the fastest, most effective way to dismantle his operation with the least risk to my family and myself.

It seemed to me that if Scott knew I was asking for an investigation into his Ponzi scheme, I had to be afraid of being murdered and I had to be concerned about being framed. If I was framed, I would lose my credibility. Either way, I would cease to be a threat to impede the massive fraud. I had to be extremely careful.

Scott used law enforcement officers to guard him while he was engaged in criminal activities. It was just one more way that he used people, instead of helping them. Here's another story about my community that shows how diametrically opposite we are from Rothstein's world of greed and selfishness.

A Call For Help

It was six A.M. and Rebecca Gerstenfeld received a call from a rabbi in the community. The rabbi told Rebecca that during the night there was a terrible fire in the community and *Sheila* was taken to the hospital without anything except her pajamas. To begin with, he asked if Rebecca could get her a skirt and a head covering and have them brought to the hospital as soon as possible. Rebecca did not have the right size skirt in the *gemach* she operated, but Raquel Benson was there making a donation of clothing and she heard what was requested. Raquel immediately dropped off her favorite skirt and a cap for Rebecca to deliver to the hospital. Later that morning Raquel saw the neighbor on the news and became aware of the extent of the tragedy. There had been a fire and one of Sheila's children had died.

No other children were injured, thank G-d, but they escaped with only the pajamas they were wearing. Sheila asked Rebecca if someone could go into the house and bring some of their clothes to them at the hospital. Rebecca made arrangements to go into the house with a few other neighbors to pry open some drawers and take all the clothes that could be recovered. Once outside, the neighbors divided up the clothes and each agreed to wash, dry, and fold them. Rebecca said she would pick up the clothes two-and-a-half hours later and deliver them to the family in the hospital.

Just as planned, Rebecca arrived to pick up the clothes and deliver them to Sheila. As the clothes were brought to the car, Rebecca saw that these were not the same clothes. She asked what had happened. She was told that even after the clothes had been washed, the smell of smoke was still there. Together, the neighbors decided to bring the clothes to the store and try to match them up with new ones of the same sizes, styles, and colors.

After the tragedy, Sheila and her family decided to go back to Seattle, the city they lived in before moving to North Miami Beach three months earlier. The funeral was scheduled in Seattle for the following morning so other neighbors quickly raised the fourteen hundred dollars needed for Sheila, her husband, and three children's trip back to Seattle. Sheila said her family loved the North Miami Beach community and were overwhelmed with the outpouring of kindness by so many people they did not even know. Since they were moving, they had a lot of furniture that they couldn't take with them. Sheila asked Rebecca if someone could locate her wedding ring and some personal documents and bring out the couple of pieces of furniture they would be taking with them. Sheila asked Rebecca if she could be sure the remaining furniture that was still intact and usable would be distributed to neighbors who could make use of it.

Rebecca's husband, Erwin, recovered the ring and passports. Then Rebecca and Erwin proceeded to find new homes for the available furniture.

Imagine – even in Sheila's tragedy, she wanted to give back to the community and thought of those in need when it came to the furniture she was not taking with her. Living in a neighborhood with people who are involved in selfless activities like this is a daily reminder of the good we can do for others when we truly care for their well-being. What a foreign concept this would be in Scottie's world.

Chapter 7

A Glimpse Back

Other things may change us,
but we start and end with family.

~ANTHONY BRANDT

T HE MELISSA BRITT LEWIS CASE certainly alarmed me, but it didn't impact my final decision one bit. As I thought about my parents' lives and my in-laws' lives, I realized that each time they faced great challenges, they acted with courage and did what was right, no matter what, because other people were important.

When I was sixteen years old, our family visited Mexico City. We had a wonderful trip but I remember a very frightening moment. I was walking down the street with my parents, my sister, and my two brothers. Suddenly we saw that across the street several boys in their late teens or early twenties were beating the living daylights out of a man. My father, Theodore J. Sakowitz (of blessed memory), immediately shouted for them to stop and began to run across the street. I became terrified as I did not think he had a chance of stopping the gang and worse; I screamed for him to come back, but he didn't. Even though he was one person without a weapon, as he approached the gang, they ran off and left the victim alone.

Later when my dad came back, I asked him why he had put

himself in such a dangerous situation. I will never forget his words: "Unless today is well-lived, tomorrow is not important" and that is exactly how he lived his entire life. He did not know what would happen to him, but he did know what would happen to the victim if he did nothing, and he viewed every person as important. I learned then and there, as scared as I was, that a person cannot just stand idly by when he has the ability to be of assistance. I wasn't sure then and I'm not even sure today that I could ever do what my father did, but remembering my father's courage and his steadfast values has given me continual direction on the proper way to live my life.

I constantly saw my father do what he thought was right and he never veered one iota from what he believed in, regardless of the consequences. Even if it meant an embarrassment, a financial loss, or even a risk to personal safety, there was right and there was wrong and there was nothing in between.

For nineteen years my father was a member of the Federal Public Defender's Office for the Southern District of Florida. He started off as the chief trial attorney for the office and within a short time became the chief assistant and for the great majority of the nineteen years, he was the federal public defender. His responsibility was to defend indigent persons, not represented by a private attorney, accused of all federal crimes from Fort Pierce to Key West. At that time, the idea of a public defender for people accused of federal crimes was almost unheard of. Since his office was one of the first few in the country, he helped mold other offices and trained countless attorneys. For two years, he served as the chairman of the Federal Public Defenders' Advisory Committee for the fifty-five federal public defenders nationwide. At one time, more defendants were prosecuted in the Southern District of Florida than in any other district in the United States. During that period, ten percent of all Federal criminal trials occurred in the district. Every assistant who worked with my father had to be compassionate, provide top quality representation, and not file pleadings that lacked merit. My father always believed in people, even when he met people who did horrible things and were heading to jail, and even when they did not believe in themselves. He knew that the day would come when they would be freed and he didn't want them to be the same person they were when they went to jail.

He started a program in his office for social workers so that the social workers could learn how the legal system and the social work field interacted, and at the same time assist his clients, instilling within them the basic knowledge they would need to function in society so as to keep these defendants from the revolving door of crime and conviction. Not surprisingly, he received letters from clients whose cases he won. But he often also received letters from prisoners or from their families thanking him for his efforts. I remember seeing many of the letters and one that especially struck me was from a person who spent many years in jail and wrote that this was the first time in his life that he had met a person who seemed to care about him. He swore that, because of that care, when he got out of jail this time he would begin caring about himself and others.

As much as my father cared about providing the best legal services possible for every person who walked into his office, it wasn't easy. The courts were busy; sometimes his office was appointed late in the game when the defendant needed a new attorney; and there wasn't always sufficient time to do the best job possible. To my father, these obstacles were unacceptable. He believed with all his heart that none of us is safe unless the worst of us are treated properly.

My father shunned publicity, but if his firm was ever criticized he personally took the case so that it was he who took the heat rather than his staff attorneys. When there was credit to be given, he stayed in the background and enjoyed watching his attorneys receive their due recognition.

There was one case in particular in which my father believed the defendant was being railroaded yet, at the risk of losing his job, he did not remain silent. There were several defendants, boxes and boxes of evidence, and tens of hours of tapes. Preparation for the trial had probably been underway for many months, if not a year or more. Unfortunately, at the last minute, an attorney representing one of the defendants disappeared.

The case was nearing the day of trial when my father's office was assigned to represent the then "unrepresented" defendant. My father assigned it to one of his assistants. When it became clear that the attorney could not handle the work, even working around the clock, in time to be prepared for trial, my father reassigned the case to himself. He asked the court for an extension of time and when that was denied, he asked the court to sever his client from the case so that the case against the other defendants could proceed and his client could be tried separately at a later date. Again the motion was denied. My father always worked day and night to help people but when *Shabbos* came, or a Jewish holiday on which work was prohibited, my father, in religious observance of such days, did not work. This case was set to go forward just after Memorial Day. Memorial Day that year was also *Shavuos*, a Jewish holiday in which work is forbidden. If it had been Memorial Day alone my father would have worked.

Just before trial each of the attorneys in the case was asked by the judge if they were ready to begin and my father stood up and announced that he was not prepared and that he could not adequately provide a defense for his client. I remember my dad telling me that he expected to pay dearly for what he did, but he was not about to allow a defendant to be railroaded just to save his job or to keep from receiving the wrath of the court. Once the record was created that the defendant's attorney was not prepared, if the case went forward against that defendant, an appellate court would likely reverse it. The judge severed the case and my father's client was tried separately.

As my father had anticipated, a hearing was held to determine if my father, because he was not prepared, should be held in contempt of court. I remember realizing what a high price my father had to pay for doing what he believed was the only proper way to conduct himself. I was ecstatic when he was found by the court not to have done anything wrong. I knew if my dad was in that situation again he would respond exactly the same way. He felt at times there were those who cared more about the appearance of justice than about justice itself, but my father cared about both and nothing was going to change his position.

However, it bothered him that the court opinion later said that he refused to work on Memorial Day and therefore had not been prepared for trial. It just wasn't true, but that was what the court opinion said. Even if he had worked that day, he would have needed weeks or months more to be adequately prepared.

Many years later I remembered what this situation said about my father's sense of hard work and his integrity, when he was diagnosed with cancer. He fought the disease valiantly, always believing that one day he would get better and return to the courtroom he loved. He was working out of his house since he was no longer able to go to our office. We found new attorneys for his fee-paying clients. He was left with only the cases he was handling pro bono. He was easily able to give away the cases that generated fees but he wasn't willing to give up cases that he was handling without charge.

The quality of his work remained as magnificent as when he was healthy. One day I saw a letter on his computer monitor that was so well written that I asked my father if I could print it out, so that he could sign it and I would send it out for him.

"No," he said, "I feel I could do better; I just don't have the energy to work on it now."

I said, "It's great, it's terrific, and it's an outstanding letter."

But he told me, "It's not my best and I always want to do my best."

It didn't seem he would ever be able to go back to court as he was dreaming he would, but within a day of *Shavuos* my father's blood count changed for the better – almost as if he was recovering. He was ready to handle a case in court and, in fact, one was scheduled in Broward County, which was about a forty-mile drive from his house in South Miami-Dade. I couldn't wait to meet him there and watch him, but the rain was so heavy, it was impossible to see the car in front of me. It seemed that everything was conspiring to stop him from getting there but he got to court and handled another case. Not long after that case, his condition deteriorated.

Something about that gnawed at me for a long time. Why was it that right after *Shavuos* my father was able to get up and go back to court even if it were for only a few days that he felt good? I wondered if it was something about *Shavuos*. I asked my father what made that day so significant to him that we had seen such a difference in his condition, but he didn't have a clue. Then I remembered that years back he was publicly embarrassed for not working on Memorial Day when in fact it was also *Shavuos*. At the time of his illness, Memorial Day on the Gregorian calendar did not come out on the same day as *Shavuos*. That year it was clearly *Shavuos* when he recovered. I looked through other papers and realized that after my father left the Federal Public Defender's Office on May 25, 1990, the day we began practicing law together was on Memorial Day, May 28, 1990, exactly a week after we formed Sakowitz & Sakowitz, Chartered. This was no coincidence, just clear proof to everyone that on Memorial Day he would work.

I felt as if it was the holiday of *Shavuos* itself that was testifying that my dad had sanctified that day, and of course he would have helped anybody on that day but for the fact that he was serving his Creator by making that day holy. It may be that on Earth it was written in the court records that my father would not prepare on Memorial Day, but I felt at that moment that in heaven it was inscribed that it was only because of *Shavuos* that my father did not show up for work. And in the end it was the heavenly court that really mattered.

My dad never wanted even a single person to fall through the cracks, but not everyone thinks that way, as can be seen by a recent incident. On January 11, 2010, *Browardbulldog.org* reported about a seventy-eight-year-old woman whose case fell through the cracks. A police officer pulled her over for driving too slowly and issued her a ticket for driving without a license or for having a revoked license. She received a notice to appear in court. Ten days after she was given the ticket she received a letter from the Department of Highway Safety and Motor Vehicles saying that her license was reinstated. The driver incorrectly thought that she no longer needed to appear in court. A few weeks later, three Broward sheriff deputies came to her home and arrested her. The next morning she, with a large group of others, appeared by video before a magistrate. The magistrate never even looked at her as he raced through the list of defendants without allowing them to speak as he confirmed their bond. This elderly woman was kept in jail for fifteen days until the prosecutor dropped the charges against her when he realized her license was not suspended.

Sadly, she appeared in court with handcuffs and shackles. There were many people who dropped the ball in this case. At least the state public defender had the strength of character to acknowledge his office's tragic mistake and to apologize. Not everyone was concerned by the horrible situation. The judge who didn't even look up or give her an opportunity to speak had this to say, according to Dan Christensen, the reporter: the judge said that he wanted to keep things in perspective. The judge explained, "It's like when FedEx delivers a million packages a day and loses one or two. Do we really want to change the whole system because of it?"

How can a judge seriously compare a person to a package? People are not something to be traded or bought. How can a judge not make eye contact with every defendant and not give every defendant an opportunity to speak? Is speed really more important than justice for every single person? Every person is important. Every person must be treated with respect! Interestingly enough, the judge in this case was a judge who asked Rothstein for his support to be appointed a judge. According to Bob Norman's interview with the judge, as posted at *The Daily Pulp* blog on January 7, 2010, Rothstein said he would speak to Governor Crist. The truth is the judge didn't need Rothstein to make the call. The judge was a fraternity brother of Governor Crist's and was on the governor's transition team.

Another great front on which my father would take heat for doing what he believed in was with taxpayers' dollars. My father believed every dollar he spent in his office had to be accounted for, and every purchase he made had to be at a fair price and for good quality. His public defender's offices were far nicer than a conventional government office, because he went out and found companies or craftsmen to provide better quality furnishings at a lower price than conventional government-issued desks and chairs.

At the end of the year, if he hadn't spent his entire budget, and that was frequently the case, he returned the balance. Many people were critical of him for doing it. They told him that, if he didn't spend the money this year, then next year his office's budget would be less. He always responded, "I can't spend the money if it is not necessary. I can't waste the taxpayers' dollars. It's not my money."

Even in my father's obituary, mention was made of his concerns over spending taxpayer money that was not necessary and that his critics thought he should spend more. There was one time when my father needed additional money for an office program and when he asked for it, he was told that because he consistently returned what he did not need, the person with authority to approve it knew that if he was asking for more, then he must really need it, and he received it.

After my father passed away, I received calls from several of his pro bono clients. They told me that they used to call my father with questions about whatever was important to them, legal matters or not. He gave them advice and then called them back at a later time to be sure that everything had worked out just fine. Each caller asked me, "Without Ted Sakowitz, who can I go to for help who would care as much?"

My father did what he did because other people are important.

My mother, Ruth Sakowitz (she should live and be well), did not face the same challenges in her life as my father; but every time a situation presented itself, it was clear that my mother acted the way she did also because she felt that other people are important.

When my mother was twelve years old, her family moved to Miami Beach, Florida, and she was shocked to see that there were two water fountains. One water fountain was for white people and one was for "colored people." Finding it so offensive that people were treated differently, from that point on my mother only drank out of the water fountain labeled for colored people. At twelve, her protest was all she thought she could do, but she wanted to align herself with what was right.

When I was in junior high, Florida schools became increasingly desegregated by the use of busing. Many white teachers went on strike and there was a shortage of teachers willing to teach, especially in the poorest, most dangerous, black neighborhoods. At the time my mother was a housewife, but highly capable of teaching, and she volunteered to teach at any school in which she was needed. She was sent to a dangerous neighborhood and she accepted that because other people are important. She noticed that most of the kids came to school without eating breakfast or having the proper nutrition. She brought cereal to school for the kids so they could start off their day with a meal. She loved the kids she taught and they loved her as well. Remarkably, her class had higher attendance *during* the strike than before the strike. After the strike ended, the principal of the school wanted to hire my mother full-time because she was making such an impact. My mother politely declined since she wasn't looking for a job.

My mother was available around the clock for anyone who came to the house, called, or needed any kind of help at all. Thanksgiving 1997 was not an easy time because my father was in the first stage of the illness that eventually claimed his incredible life. For years, my mother prepared a beautiful meal for all the women of her Amit chapter on the Wednesday before or after Thanksgiving. Even in her mid-sixties, she was one of the youngest members in her chapter.

The meal – which was part of a membership drive and a fundraiser – was different every year, and all of the desserts were freshly baked. As became her custom, she made far more than enough food because all of the ladies loved to take some home for their husbands. And the occasion was more than just lunch. My mother collected all kinds of gift items so that everyone left happily with a great prize.

That year we begged our mother to cancel the event. We felt that she was just not in a position to focus on cooking for so many people when her whole world was turned upside down.

"Absolutely not," my mother responded. "They look forward to this luncheon. It's a fundraising opportunity that makes money for our projects in Israel, which help children. I will not take it away from them."

So we suggested that all the food and desserts be bought this time.

Again my mother said, "Absolutely not. Everyone looks forward to a home-cooked meal and freshly cooked baked goods."

That membership luncheon was no different. My mother stayed up all night cooking and baking, because other people are important. As always, it was a beautiful and well-attended meal. As people left with their prizes, they also filled Styrofoam containers my mother put out. My mother asked the guests to please take something home because she did not want any leftovers. Even for that membership luncheon, my mother cooked double the amount needed (again because other people are important, and they loved it). To this day, more than a dozen years later, my mother still makes that same fundraising luncheon for Amit, and they still love it.

The lessons I learned from my in-laws were no different. My father-in-law, Benzion Leibowitz (of blessed memory), lost his entire family – except one sister – including his parents, aunts, uncles, other sisters, brothers, nieces, and nephews in the Holocaust. As painful as the experience was, he focused his attention on helping others. During the war, he was in the Munkaszolgálat, a forced labor camp.

Most of the assigned tasks were for unnecessary services like digging ditches and carrying stones in the mountains. The work was difficult and many did not survive; prisoners not able to keep up were shot and killed without a second thought. As the war was ending, my father-in-law concocted a plan to escape, but he shared his plan with others. He knew it would be safer to escape by himself, but he felt it was worth the additional risk to try to save others at the same time. The plan was successful and he escaped, providing himself the opportunity to spend his years helping other people, even though he had to move to Canada, where he didn't know the language or the culture. Before the move to Canada to live near his sister, my father-in-law made his way to Israel where he joined the Haganah (the underground Jewish militia that became the national army of Israel) to join in the fight for Israel's independence. He was honored to help defend his fellow brethren and the State of Israel in its making.

My mother-in-law, Clara Leibowitz (she should live and be well), suffered much greater tragedies at the hands of Hitler (G-d should wipe out his name). Her parents, brother-in-law, and most of her cousins, aunts, and uncles were killed during the Holocaust. They arrived at Auschwitz on June 6, 1944, at 2:30 P.M. Dr. Joseph Mengele, known as "the angel of death," stood in front of them and said in German, "daughter away from mommy."

Mengele, with white gloves covering his hands, tapped my mother-in-law, then a twenty-one-year-old young lady, on her shoulder and sent her in one direction and her parents in the other. That was the last time she saw her parents. At midnight she was stripped, all of the hair shaved from her body, disinfected, and issued clothes to wear. At four A.M. the next morning, my mother-in-law was required to walk four-and-a-half kilometers from Auschwitz to Birkenau. Before the start of the hike, a vicious guard said she liked my mother-in-law's shoes and took them, forcing her to walk barefoot on the rough terrain. The entire road was constructed out of tombstones from Jewish cemeteries. The stones were broken and jagged.

My mother-in-law was forced from one death camp to another, starting with Auschwitz, then Kaisenwald, followed by camps in Riga, Lybau, Spilve, and Dondanga near the Baltic Sea. From there she went back to the Reich – with a stop at the Stutthof camp and at a camp at Leipzig, and finally to Schönau where she and those with her ate and slept in an empty military barracks consisting of twenty-eight wooden built rooms with one pool and one washroom. In Leipzig, she worked at ATG, an underground aircraft production facility. She was responsible for holding sheet metal in place and stepping on a pedal, thus causing two screws at a time to be driven into the sheet metal airplane parts. It was grueling work that stretched from six A.M. to six P.M.

Albert Bröme, a limping German officer, was the floor supervisor. He once pointed to the rafters and said that was where he would hang her if she ever again mentioned what she might do with her life once she was freed.

Notwithstanding these conditions, my mother-in-law took the opportunity to clean the kitchen each night from about nine P.M. to one A.M. at Schönau. As tired as she was, she was glad to do it since it positioned her to be able to help others. Each night she took out a bucket of soup and a ladle to fill the empty cans of her hungry fellow prisoners. She also snuck cooked potatoes in her clothes and secretly passed them out.

The thoughts of how my father and father-in-law lived their lives and how my mother and mother-in-law continue to live their lives only strengthened my resolve on what had to be done about Scott Rothstein. I knew that how our children respond to challenges they face in the future would be based in large part upon how my wife and I live our lives and respond to situations we encounter; we are their most important role models and, in taking down Rothstein, I wanted to set a fine example as our parents had done for us.

The question of how this should be done, however, was still not clear.

Neither my neighbors in the story I call "A Wedding Long Remembered" nor Rothstein, could afford an expensive wedding. Unlike Rothstein who spent hundreds of thousands of dollars of stolen money for a wedding, my neighbors chose to spend within their means. The story is proof that with the help of those around you, you can have a lovely wedding that honors the union of two people, and does not mortgage your future.

A Wedding Long Remembered

Almost a year ago we danced at Tamar's wedding. It brought back memories of twenty-eight years earlier when I danced at the wedding of her parents, Reuven and Hadassah Swerdlik. Theirs is still regarded as one of the most memorable weddings in our community. Harold and Brenda Levenson's backyard was the ideal location for the Swerdliks' wedding. It was large with a lush, manicured lawn and a permanent frame of a *succah* (hut) that was easily transformed into a *chuppah* (wedding canopy). Most of their friends lived within a few blocks and the weather was perfect for an outdoor ceremony. In an age when flowers often cost thousands of dollars for a large wedding that takes years to pay off, the bride, Hadassah Swerdlik, paid cash. True, it was only thirty-five dollars. But even in 1982, that was not a lot of money for wedding flowers. Mind you, the thirty-five dollars included delivery! The roses, daisies, and baby's breath were ordered the day of the wedding and included a bouquet as well as flowers to decorate the *chuppah*.

The cost of a wedding is a major expense by any standard, so I am sure you're beginning to understand that this wedding was not remembered for being the most lavish and expensive, and for good reason. The groom, Reuven, and the bride, Hadassah, were both in college and did not expect their parents to pay for the wedding. Theirs was a community wedding in which everyone was involved, and it was quite lively. Before the ceremony, homemade hors d'oeuvres were prepared by the hosts and served by guests. *Rebbetzin* Leff made the *challahs*.

The newly renovated and expanded social hall at Young Israel (the *shul*) had just been completed. After the wedding ceremony, the affair continued there, just five blocks away. A one-man band provided the music. The Swerdliks ordered chicken, and the balance of the food, including the wedding cake, was prepared by friends. The paper cups and plastic plates and cutlery were provided by friends. The community and the Swerdliks proved that a memorable wedding is more about celebrating with good friends and family than about spending a great deal of money.

Getting back to the basics and using community facilities and neighbors' backyards can result in a meaningful and memorable wedding, and is a practical solution when a bride and groom, and their families, don't have the means to fund an expensive affair. Not only did the Swerdliks' wedding illustrate what is really important about a wedding, it showed how our community's leaders differ from so-called leaders like Scott Rothstein.

Rabbi Zev Leff performed the wedding ceremony, *and* he was one of three moving men who helped the Swerdliks go from two apartments to a new one by packing and moving their furniture and boxes. Rabbi Leff used a hand truck and loaded all of the boxes from Reuven's apartment into his station wagon and drove the vehicle to the couple's new apartment and unloaded the contents!

Helping out has always been a hallmark of Rabbi Leff. He is the same Rabbi Leff who today is a well known and highly respected Torah scholar in Israel and finds time to teach at several seminaries as well as at the *yeshiva* where he is the dean. He is involved with several other programs and still makes time to answer questions and provide guidance to the many who count on him. In addition, he finds time to keep up with his close friends and the Swerdliks are counted high among his friends.

In 2008 and 2009, the Swerdliks' two youngest children, fifteen-year-old Shira and thirteen-year-old Esther, went to camp in Israel. On a *Shabbos* on which the campers were permitted to leave camp and stay with a family, the teacher asked the girls where they were going for *Shabbos*. Shira answered, "To Rabbi Leff's."

The teacher said, "It is beautiful that you are going to Rabbi Leff's community, Moshav Matisyahu. But which family are you staying with?"

Shira answered, "Rabbi Leff."

The teacher asked the Swerdlik girls who was going to pick them up, and again the answer was, "Rabbi Leff."

Still not finding this answer believable, the teacher was stunned as the recognized giant in the world of Torah, Rabbi Leff, drove up in his car and called for Shira and Esther to hop in.

In my neighborhood, a leader does not separate himself from the people in the community. He immerses himself in the day-to-day lives of his congregants. He doesn't wield power in order to raise his standing; he focuses his energy on helping his community grow spiritually while not ignoring their worldly needs. Our leaders influence us through their good deeds, acts of kindness, and knowledge.

Chapter 8

Process of Elimination

*Right is right, even if everyone
is against it; and wrong is wrong,
even if everyone is for it.*

~WILLIAM PENN

THE FIRST OPTION on my list of possible law enforcement agencies to contact, and the first one I needed to take off that list, was the Sheriff of Broward County. It was not because I had anything personally against Sheriff Al Lamberti. In fact, I didn't know him and I had never heard anything negative about him. I assumed he was an outstanding person and an effective sheriff, and that all of his deputies were also hardworking honest men and women, but a cloud of suspicion hung over that office.

First, the disgraced former sheriff, Ken Jenne, went to work for RRA about a week after his discharge from federal prison after being convicted on corruption charges. In Broward County, a sheriff is elected, and I had read that Scott Rothstein directly or indirectly was responsible for one donation being made from his Bova restaurant partner to an Electioneering Communications Organization supporting Al Lamberti's campaign for election to sheriff in the amount of $150,000. A second donation, of $60,000, for the benefit of Lamberti came from Rothstein's law partner Stuart Rosenfeldt. The final $50,000 was from another Rothstein company. Interestingly, Rosenfeldt also indirectly contributed $90,000 to Lamberti's opponent; and David Boden, Rothstein's in-house counsel, indirectly contributed $70,000 to Lamberti's opponent. It certainly seemed that influence in the Broward Sheriff's Office was more important than who the sheriff was.

Even though I did not learn of anything that was promised to Rothstein for the donation, there was certainly the appearance of improper influence by having former Sheriff Ken Jenne at RRA and having so much money funneled to support Al Lamberti's election bid. In fact, the Sheriff's picture hung in Scott Rothstein's office and on it was a beautiful handwritten note to Scott. My concern was that Scott Rothstein's connection to the Sheriff and the Sheriff's Office was so intimate that, if an investigation were launched through the Sheriff's Office, someone could mention it to Scott, either intentionally or not. So many people were blinded by what a great person Scott appeared to be that if an investigation was conducted, they would think this investigation was nonsense since Rothstein was a man whose reputation was beyond reproach. For all of those reasons, the Sheriff of Broward County was the first choice I eliminated.

I was smart to do so; only months later it was revealed that when Rothstein fled to Morocco as his scam was surfacing, it was the Sheriff's executive assistant, Lt. David Benjamin, whom Rothstein called to personally usher him to his waiting jet to leave the country, and Lt. Benjamin obliged. Benjamin also apparently started a consulting business, DWB Consulting. It seems he received $30,000 from Rothstein. Rothstein was also a member of the Broward Sheriff's Advisory Council. These additional items confirmed my earlier reason for concern.

Next on my list was the Fort Lauderdale Police Department (FLPD), but I had concerns there as well. I had read on Internet blogs and online media that Scott Rothstein's office, house, and even his restaurant, Bova Prime, were guarded by high-ranking, off-duty Fort Lauderdale police officers. On my first and third visits to

Rothstein's office, I noticed the presence of a Fort Lauderdale police officer; it just seemed too cozy an arrangement. Since the officers were working their regular shift at FLPD and working on the side for Rothstein, that meant they were working more than a forty-hour week. In addition, they were not paid by the FLPD for working these hours, but by Rothstein. That would mean that there could have been thirty-to-fifty or more different officers, each taking up an eight-hour shift once or more a week for Rothstein. I wasn't about to take a chance that thirty-to-fifty high-ranking officers in the department might learn of an investigation being launched against their employer, Scottie Rothstein, especially since they didn't seem to really be providing security for the firm or even Rothstein. I say that since the police officer was only stationed outside Rothstein's office. He was not near the main door or on the other RRA floor to which I went. The guard just seemed to be there to give credibility to Rothstein's scam much like the rest of the scenery. There was no metal detector to go through to enter Rothstein's office, nor did the officer ask if I was carrying any weapon, or even for any identification. On my second visit, I did not even see him. It was particularly odd that an agency trained to sniff out fraud was guarding a fraudster.

In reality, the only one who really needed the police protection was Frank Adderley, the Fort Lauderdale police chief, for his home and especially his bedroom. Four months after his department started providing round-the-clock police presence at Rothstein's home and office, the police chief ran from his Plantation home dodging bullets from his own wife. Apparently the chief's wife, Eleanor, was not very pleased with her husband's alleged cheating on her or his buying his alleged girlfriend a nicer Christmas gift than he bought her.

Integrity is important, but even the appearance of integrity cannot be overstated. The public needs to have confidence in the government and, in particular, law enforcement. I am sad to say that based solely on the dozens of officers being assigned to Scott Rothstein, I did not have the confidence I needed to provide information I believed would lead to an investigation of Scott Rothstein.

My gut feelings about the FLPD were reinforced later when it became known that Fort Lauderdale Police Chief Frank Adderley dined weekly and possibly daily at one of Rothstein's restaurants, Bova Prime, and attended several Dolphins games in Rothstein's luxury box at Land Shark (now known as Sun Life) Stadium. Adderley even flew with Rothstein on a private plane to a Dolphins game in New York at the Jets' Stadium. He also attended large gatherings at Rothstein's mansion four different times. According to a December 1, 2009, *SunSentinel.com* article by Brittany Wallman, Adderley said he always paid for his meals at Bova Prime and covered the cost of the football games he attended with Rothstein. That said, how could there be no undue influence going on?

The third agency I eliminated was the Florida Bar Association. This was not because I didn't trust the members of the Florida Bar, and not because I did not have the highest respect for them. The problem was that there were just too many attorneys in high positions who had a relationship with Scott Rothstein. He was a member of the nominating committee for the Fourth District Court of Appeals, and so he was the person with whom attorneys rubbed elbows with if they wanted to become judges. I was concerned that if I made a complaint about his activity and asked the Bar to investigate his trust accounts, and anybody tipped him off, I would be eliminated. I was afraid for my life. This would be the case even if I were to make my complaint anonymously because I feared Scott would easily find out who turned him in. He was just that well connected.

Since I believed by this time that Scott Rothstein's sale of settlement agreements was entirely fabricated, I was concerned that each potential investor had been given slightly different facts. If I kept my information too general it may not have received the attention it deserved, but if I made my information very specific, I was pretty much leaving my fingerprints even if my name was not revealed. All I needed to do was mention information that was only known by me, and Scott would know right away who filed the complaint.

After I eliminated the Florida Bar Association, there were six options left. The Securities and Exchange Commission appeared not to pose a risk of being infiltrated by Scott Rothstein. However, certainly after the Bernie Madoff and Allen Sanford debacles, it was not an agency known for working at warp speed, and oftentimes it would only get involved if no other agency took responsibility Even then its involvement was often futile. I imagined that any possible Rothstein investigation would center on whether, in fact, selling a settlement agreement amounted to the sale of a security and, if it was not, the SEC would not get involved. If it was, then at some point it would get involved. Because of lack of speed, and its recent showing of ineffectiveness, I eliminated this choice.

The next choice to be eliminated was the Internal Revenue Service. Again, I believed that the IRS was unlikely to have been infiltrated by Rothstein's organization, but I was concerned with speed, as collecting tax dollars due is not as high a priority as stopping thieves from stealing money.

With five governmental agencies eliminated, I was then faced with the possibility of going to the media. One investigative reporter relentless in his pursuit of Scott Rothstein was Bob Norman with the *Broward/Palm Beach New Times*. Norman wrote for its blog, *The Daily Pulp*. Norman was undoubtedly on Scott's case but didn't seem to know exactly what Scott was doing wrong. However, he knew Scott was up to something. He believed the RRA law firm was a "house of cards that would eventually collapse." He mentioned the number of cars Scott had, the real estate he owned, the contributions he gave to charity, and the contributions he gave to politicians. In Norman's mind, it didn't add up, and he wasn't about to let go of Scott. He knew a person could not be earning what Scott was earning and spending what Scott must have been spending in a legitimate way. Norman saw the smoke and his eyes were open looking for the flames.

On September 8, 2009, Norman wrote of a phone call he received on August 25, 2009, from Rothstein. Norman told of how the chairman of RRA threatened to "destroy him." Rothstein, Norman said, was seething and said, "He was going to sue me and my wife [*Sun-Sentinel* staff writer Brittany Wallman] and bankrupt our household. It was sort of the phone-call version of being mugged by a gang of hooligans in Central Park."

Norman had a penchant for going after crooked politicians and the people who helped corrupt them. As Rothstein started purchasing interests in companies doing business with the government, he was caught on Norman's radar. Norman saw the ownership of companies by Rothstein and politicians, and added to that fact the influence of the lobbyists from RRA as well as the large amounts of money Rothstein was spreading to politicians. Norman smelled a rat and refused to remain silent. As he began to dig, Rothstein came after him swinging.

The very next day after the threatening phone call, September 9, 2009, Norman changed his tune and seemed apologetic, writing:

> Sure, someone who hits the big time like Rothstein is going to get tongues wagging, but don't believe any of the talk without proof …. The guy has his hand in several businesses and owns a thriving law firm. Don't hate him just because he can buy the Versace mansion. That he went ballistic on me makes for an interesting story, and you can take from it what you will, but it certainly proves that Rothstein cares immensely for his work and friends.
>
> … I'm always skeptical and will always be vigilant watching the firm's political interests, but I think it's time for a whole lot of people to start giving Rothstein the benefit of the doubt.

Norman must have written those words in utter frustration after seeing so much manure and knowing there had to be a horse, even if he didn't see one. Maybe he even believed there was a small chance that Rothstein was legitimate. If he did, it must have been a very small chance, but nonetheless a chance. With that, he wasn't prepared to be sued without having the goods on Rothstein. If any reporter was ready for the information I had, it was Bob Norman.

I thought a quick email to Bob Norman would result in a story that would bring an abrupt halt to the criminal activity of Scott Rothstein and have him arrested before another dime could be removed from his account. Norman's story would probably have seemed like an oddball theory to many, but also a perfect explanation of why Scott could spend what he was spending.

If Norman listed each of the red flags that I would identify, I didn't think it would take long for word to spread to every agency near and far to have his firm on their radar. I also thought that each attorney in the firm would be writing to everyone else in the firm to determine the truth of the allegations. BlackBerry devices would be going off like never before. Every ostrich within the firm would immediately pull his head out of the sand and realize that he could no longer just mind his own business and ignore how the firm was growing. Each attorney would have to examine how the business interests, buildings, cars, and homes were being purchased by the CEO. It was like a game of Monopoly, except the money was real, and there seemed to be a disproportionate number of people landing on free parking and winning the jackpot. Soon they might imagine that the "go directly to jail" cards were fairly common and everyone would be trying to locate the "get out of jail free" cards. Those who had been getting reimbursed for political contributions, especially unusually large ones, would need to start lawyering up.

It seemed like the perfect solution, as it would be quick, take one email, and within twenty-four-to-forty-eight hours halt the illegal operation. In addition, the risk to me would be minimal. The danger was that even though I was more than ninety percent sure that Rothstein was the kingpin of a Ponzi scheme and, even if I was wrong about the Ponzi scheme, it was most likely some other illegal activity such as money laundering, I understood that there still remained the possibility that I was wrong. Accordingly, if I were wrong, the reputation of Scottie Rothstein and RRA would be wrongly and unjustly ruined, as would mine. I could not take that chance, and therefore I could not go with this option, no matter how good it seemed.

With six options down and only three remaining, I thought that rather than emailing Bob Norman and getting word all over town, I could go to the RRA website and copy all the attorneys' email addresses and email them each a letter. I wouldn't use my own email address and I wouldn't even use my own computer. It would be too easy to trace. I thought I could go to a location where computers could be rented and I could pay for it with cash so my identity would not be known. A new email address could be created in minutes and I could email the entire firm at once. I would be less specific as to the details since I would not want my fingerprints to appear. The letter would quite simply point out that Scott Rothstein was selling tens of millions of dollars of pre-lawsuit settlements and/or he claimed to have an enormous volume of these for sale. I would suggest that the volume of claims was absurd and this appeared to be a Ponzi scheme, and I would apologize for being light on facts but I did not want my identity known.

I imagined BlackBerry devices going off and each person calling or emailing the next. Within minutes, the firm's labor and employment department would be deluged with inquiries as to whether or not it was handling a high volume of cases that are settled without filing a suit and then sold to investors. Expecting that the answer would be in the negative, attorneys would make a beeline to Rothstein's office. Others would insist on getting bank balances directly from the bank. Soon every agency I wanted to contact would be asked to freeze the funds and there would be utter chaos at the firm. Again, within twenty-four–forty-eight hours there would be a sudden halt to all illegal activities. Scott Rothstein would be in custody and no more money would be taken to the bank or stolen from investors.

Like the previous option, it would be fast, effective, and a minimal risk to my family and me. I would even be able to go to different locations to use computers and answer any necessary questions without having to disclose my identity. However, the same drawback as writing to Bob Norman existed: what if, despite all the evidence, I was wrong?

I now had only two choices left. Each seemed to have an advantage and a disadvantage. The first was contacting the Florida attorney general by telephone; this seemed to be a good option because I had heard that the attorney general was investigating a matter with Scott Rothstein and that gave me confidence that the attorney general would focus on this matter. The enemy of my enemy is my friend, or so goes the expression. I wanted to go to the attorney general. I thought it was a good option. My concern was that there was just too much money flowing in and out of the campaigns of the governor and the attorney general, and money blurs vision. Someone in the attorney general's office could learn of the investigation and if it was someone who believed in Scott Rothstein, or someone who just believed in money, he or she could pass on the information. Regrettably, I found myself concerned about dealing with agencies to which money was flowing since large amounts of money had to create an expectation of a return on the investment. As I have written many times, I did not know of any misconduct or inappropriate conduct by any of the agencies, but when a lot of money is flowing from the person being investigated, it creates a cloud of suspicion that made me afraid to put my life on the line.

By default, I was left with only one choice: the Federal Bureau of Investigation. Since the director of the FBI is not elected and since the agents are not out soliciting political contributions, I felt my personal risk was greatly diminished. Scott Rothstein had mentioned that he had many former law enforcement agents on his staff and I didn't know if that statement was true or was just meant to intimidate or impress me. If it were true, I had no way of knowing with which agencies they were. If they had been with the FBI, I was about to make a very bad choice. However, since there were no better choices and since I didn't know whether former law enforcement officers, other than former Broward Sheriff Ken Jenne, were employed by RRA (and if they were, whether any of them had been with the FBI), I concluded that that agency was the least likely to have been penetrated by Rothstein. I decided the best thing to do was to call anonymously. I wasn't going to be so paranoid as to wonder if the FBI could see the caller ID even with my phone blocked.

Later, the thirty-seven page indictment filed by the Acting United States Attorney for the Southern District of Florida regarding Scott Rothstein substantiated my fears. It read, "Ponzi scheme funds were also used to provide gratuities to high-ranking members of police agencies in order to curry favor with such police personnel and to deflect law enforcement scrutiny of the activities of RRA and defendant Rothstein."

No mention was made of which agencies received the funds.

My caution concerning blowing the whistle more or less publicly and winding up being wrong was borne out of my concern for the resulting embarrassment and scandal to Rothstein and RRA if I was wrong. In my community, neighbors go out of the way to avoid embarrassment to others even when they are not the cause of it. With that context in mind, enjoy this story that I call "Sorry, Wrong Number."

Sorry, Wrong Number

Rabbi *Jonathan Cohen* was advertising to hire an employee. *Herbert Schwartz* heard about the position available and called Rabbi Cohen. After Herbert introduced himself, he mentioned he was calling about the available position but asked that his inquiry be kept confidential. He said he was embarrassed that he needed a position and had not yet been able to find one. Rabbi *Ari Cohen* realized that Herbert intended to call Rabbi Jonathan Cohen, not him. He quickly looked up the other Rabbi Cohen's phone number and he asked Herbert if he could call him back on his "office line" a little bit later. Herbert said he could, and Ari Cohen speedily called Jonathan Cohen and explained the situation so that the correct Rabbi Cohen could finish the conversation without Mr. Schwartz being humiliated.

Were these steps necessary? Yes, of course, if you place importance on an individual's dignity and you understand that embarrassing a person can be devastating to a person's self-esteem. My neighbors are willing to take many steps, if necessary, to avoid hurting anyone, no matter how minor that hurt might seem to an outsider.

Chapter 9

A Moment of Clarity

*It is not what we get. But who we
become, what we contribute...
that gives meaning to our lives.*

~ANTHONY ROBBINS

AT THIS POINT I had understood that the most effective way for me to stop Scott Rothstein from defrauding anyone else was to contact the FBI. Before doing so, however, I needed clarity that I had done everything possible to be sure that my information and analysis was as accurate as it could be. I called my rabbi to discuss my intentions. Rabbi Shapiro felt that because of the magnitude of the situation I should contact one of the greatest *Torah* scholars of our generation, and he suggested *Rav* Shmuel Kaminensky.

I called *Rav* Shmuel, as he is known. After I explained the situation, he told me I should do everything within my power to prevent others from being harmed by Mr. Rothstein. "Every human being," he said, "is precious, and their money is precious as well." He said I was correct in recognizing that I could not stand by and allow other people to lose their money if it was able to be prevented.

Rav Shmuel cautioned me to be mindful that I could be wrong, and, therefore, to do everything possible to be sure that neither Mr.

Rothstein nor the firm was harmed should there be a legal explana-
tion for what I perceived to be illegal. He said to act quickly and
not to wait until I gathered further proof. He felt that I had enough
cause to believe Mr. Rothstein was a danger to the public. The call
ended with *Rav* Shmuel giving me his blessings.

My next call was to the FBI. Quite nervous, I first blocked my
phone number and then called my office phone from my cell phone
to see if my number appeared. When it didn't, I dialed the FBI's
North Miami-Dade County, Florida Office. I explained why I was
calling and my call was then forwarded to the appropriate person.
I explained that I had become aware of a situation that I believed
posed a great danger to society and I needed the FBI's assistance.

I gave a basic description of the situation and discussed in detail
the red flags that I could not overcome. The analyst with whom
I spoke asked me many questions. At one point he suggested that it
sounded like Rothstein was engaged in extorting money. I agreed it
sounded like it, but I did not believe that the claims Scott was brag-
ging about really existed. After further questions, the analyst asked
me my name. At that point I indicated I would prefer to remain
anonymous. He assured me it was my right but he asked if I would
consider giving my name since the information I provided seemed
very credible. He explained that agents may have questions for me
and that the matter was just too important for me to not be able to
be reached.

My suggestion was, "How about you save up your questions and
I'll call you back at a day and time you designate? At that point I'll
answer whatever questions there are and if you think you need to
speak to me again I could call at a future date."

That wasn't what the FBI was looking for. The analyst asked if
I would at least give my phone number.

I laughed and said, "I have a funny feeling that if I give the FBI
my phone number I'm sure they can figure out who I am." My
reason for not wanting to give my name was that as long as Scott

Rothstein continued to operate with business as usual, I felt as if I were in danger. I explained that so many politicians, celebrities, sports figures, law enforcement officers, and even heads of charities had leveraged their credibility with Scott; my concern was that everyone in Broward believed in him. He had the seal of approval from everyone who was anyone and if an investigation came up and my name was leaked out, I could become toast. After further discussion and being assured that if anything went wrong and if Rothstein were to remain in operation, my identity would be protected. I provided my name and telephone number.

Once the analyst was finished asking me questions, I asked his last name so I would know who to ask for if I needed to call back. Interesting enough, he said, "I am not permitted to give out my last name." He told me to mark down the day and time I called and give his first name and with that information the agency would know with whom I spoke.

When I got off the telephone, I knew I had done the right thing. I even felt that by giving my name I did what was best for my country, even though it may not have been best for me, though I tried to quell my budding paranoia. The next morning as I walked outside, I found myself looking at the corner to make sure that there were not any Fort Lauderdale police cars, Broward County sheriff's cars or any other vehicles I didn't recognize. As I walked down the block to *shul* and saw that there were not any strange cars at either end of the block, or anywhere in between, I felt a sense of relief. Then, I started to think to myself, what if there were cars, what would I do? What if a policeman pulled me over? I could disappear or I could be framed. If I was lucky, I thought maybe they would just beat me up as a warning. After calling the FBI, if I saw a strange car with someone in it near my house – that signaled danger. If I saw a Fort Lauderdale police car or Broward County sheriff's car near my house or near my car, for me that signaled danger. If I was driving down the street and I saw red and blue flashing lights behind me, I considered that a danger, too.

I hoped the FBI would take immediate action and I expected to read in the paper within a few days that Rothstein was under arrest, or better yet, that I would receive a call telling me that I had made a big mistake. But I knew it was still worth calling the FBI. Perhaps I would be told there was a logical explanation for everything and all Scott was doing was exaggerating, that his activity had not reached the level of "criminal."

What I absolutely expected was that the FBI would send an agent to Rothstein's firm posing as a client who was sexually harassed by an employer. I envisioned the agent asking about the employment law group's experience, the number of cases it handled annually, the percent that settled prior to filing suit, and the typical settlement amount of the cases. Armed with information I had provided to the FBI, I anticipated that a couple of agents would have contacted Akbar at the phone number I provided, expressing interest in investing. From there I anticipated that a meeting with Rothstein would be scheduled and inquiries similar to mine would be made. If the employment law group indicated that less than a handful of cases were settled for half-a-million dollars or more without a lawsuit and Rothstein suggested over 3,000 per year were being settled, the FBI would start to recognize the problem. They would then immediately obtain a warrant to monitor the bank accounts and tap the phones. Other agents would likely contact other major employment law firms in the area and inquire as to the volume of cases those firms were handling. In particular they would be interested in the number of cases in which the opposing party was represented by an RRA attorney. It wouldn't take long to recognize the problem and protect the public.

Then again, I thought, none of this might happen, or if it did happen, it might not be quick. I began to realize that this process could take weeks or months or even possibly half a year. I could not imagine looking over my shoulder for half a year. I couldn't imagine the tens of millions of dollars a week that would continue to pour into Scottie's scam. I couldn't imagine what I had to prepare for. Often I woke up in the middle of the night and found myself pacing up and back in the living room, re-running the events in my mind, wondering what else I could do. I began to question whether it was my responsibility to contact the labor department of RRA and several other firms. In the end, I concluded the information I provided to the FBI was sufficient to warrant an investigation. After all, that is why we have law enforcement agencies.

If I felt that I was in immediate danger, the first of the two law enforcement officers I was going to call was my neighbor, Sergeant Nelson Reyes, Jr. He is one of the most courageous police officers I have ever met. Sergeant Reyes does not just live in my neighborhood, my neighborhood lives in him. When there is trouble and commotion, most people's instincts direct them to run for cover. Not Nelson's. He has distinguished himself as a leader who rushes to the trouble, knowing his involvement could save lives.

The second number I kept handy was that of Major Mark D. Jeter, the police officer responsible for the portion of Miami-Dade County in which I live. He is a very efficient, organized, and effective leader who communicates well with members of the different communities he serves. He is very visible and accessible. Though he is in charge of a large portion of Miami-Dade County, he gives out his cell phone number and email address generously. He works hard to build good relations with all organized neighborhoods in his district that want to partner with the police to make their communities safer. If Sergeant Reyes and Major Jeter were both unavailable or if I were in an area out of the jurisdiction of both, I would call 9-1-1.

I made up my mind that if the police pulled me over I would slow down but I wouldn't stop the vehicle unless there were at least three or four police cars. If I had to stop, I would stop but I would open my window only an inch to give my driver's license and I would not roll down the window any further or get out of the car without three or four police officers being present. I was too concerned that if Rothstein knew I went to the FBI, something could happen to me. I could be pulled over for an ordinary traffic stop, or for speeding, or for making a rolling right-hand turn, and an officer could plant drugs on my seat and say that he found them in my car. If that happened, I expected nobody would believe me and I would soon be out of Scott's way. I believed that with three-or-four police officers together it would be far less likely that all would be willing to lie.

I hoped that not even one police officer would lie but I understood how much money Scott had to spread around. I saw the cloud of suspicion that hung over Broward and I was not about to risk my life more than necessary. Rothstein knew how to entice people to do what he wanted, legal or not. Amazingly, so many people willingly and sheepishly surrendered their own good judgment for the promise of unreasonably high rewards. I saw up close the unbelievable power of greed. I was living what I had previously only seen in frightening books and movies. I understood that with enough money even law enforcement employees could be bought.

If I called Sergeant Reyes or Major Jeter or 9-1-1, I would explain quickly that I was too scared to stop. I'd explain to them that I had provided certain information about a well-connected Ponzi schemer to the FBI and now I was too paranoid to stop. I'd explain that I was not hiding or running but was just afraid of being killed or framed and I would respectfully request that other police officers be present. I hadn't been pulled over by a police officer in many years so I doubted I would be pulled over, but if I were, I probably would be paranoid. Being pulled over after so many years without being stopped, and to happen as soon as I called the FBI – that would be too much of a coincidence. I knew there was a risk of being arrested by planning to do what I did. But somehow, being arrested didn't seem anywhere near as frightening as being killed or framed, especially when I thought of the gruesome details of the Melissa Britt Lewis case.

If I felt even the slightest threat against my family, I decided that my wife and children would need to move to my wife's triplet sister's house in New Jersey until this whole situation resolved itself. It pained me to think that my daughters in tenth grade and twelfth grade, who are so active in school, would just have to disappear and give up the things that they were working hard to accomplish. My son would also have to leave and he would need to choose a graduate school out of town. We also have a daughter in college in Israel and one in graduate school in New York. They wouldn't be displaced, but they are both of marriageable age. I wondered how one makes a wedding with many guests while in hiding.

My wife is a pharmacist licensed only in Florida. In the current poor real estate environment, her check comes in handy and the insurance benefits are nice as well. With the slow economy, I wasn't so sure that if we had to go into hiding, her employer would give her a leave of absence; especially if it was for four-to-six months. I wasn't sure where I would get insurance or how I would replace her paycheck, but those were the least of my problems. My goal was to make it through each day and to get home safely. I knew there was a price to be paid for living in an exceptional country and that, as much as I didn't like it, it was a price well worth paying for the privilege of living in America and helping to keep it great.

The time between my call to the FBI and Scott's arrest was a very tense period for me, but it became even more chilling when I realized that I couldn't sit still and wait for the FBI to put a stop to the highflying Scott Rothstein. I had to speak up any time I could when I knew other people were investing or considering investing. But I had to balance trying to protect other people from being defrauded with trying to stay alive.

My call to the FBI was just before Yom Kippur, the Day of Atonement. That year Rothstein was busy getting large amounts of dough anywhere he could. I remembered that the year before, someone in my neighborhood was also looking for people with dough – albeit a very different kind – in the story I call "Special Kneads for the Eve of Yom Kippur."

Special Kneads For the Eve of Yom Kippur

Traditionally, it is auspicious for a complete recovery from an illness when forty women have in mind the same person's recovery when they are "separating the *challah*" and making a blessing. Each of the women prepares *challahs* (loaves of rich bread prepared especially for *Shabbos* and Jewish holidays) with five pounds of dough (enough to bake four–five *challahs*). They can keep the *challahs* for themselves or give them to others. When a woman bakes *challahs*, she recites a blessing, and takes off a small piece of dough before shaping the remainder. She burns the separated piece in the oven.

Natalie Gross sought to organize a group of forty women who were baking *challahs* for the evening before Yom Kippur for this magnanimous goal of a full recovery. Four-year-old Rucama Aliza was the neighbor for whom everyone was praying. She was and until this day is on life support. The community was giving extra charity and saying extra prayers asking G-d for her speedy and full recovery. After Natalie Gross got the word out, more than one hundred women around the world emailed Natalie with their desire to participate as well.

What better way to begin the holy day, Yom Kippur? Not only is the *challah* baked fresh for the feast before the holiday, but even the thoughts and blessings one has are for a recovery for another person, perhaps even a person one does not know. What better way to go before the Master of the universe on the Day of Atonement than finishing a meal at a table graced by such special *challahs*?

Before a religious Jew eats any food, he makes a blessing. I once heard that the difference between an ordinary and a great religious Jew is that the ordinary religious Jew makes a blessing so that he can eat the apple he desires. A great religious Jew, on the other hand, eats the apple so that he can make the blessing he so much desires to make. What could be said of a person who elects to bake a *challah* so that she can participate with others in praying that the separating of the *challah* could help another person? When a people begin to add such holiness to everything they do for the merit of another, one starts to understand how the world is supposed to run.

Chapter 10

Spreading the Word Quietly

*Successful people are always looking
for opportunities to help others.
Unsuccessful people are always asking,
"What's in it for me?"*

~BRIAN TRACY

BEFORE I CALLED THE FBI, a broker, *Adam Davis*, called me to pitch Scott's settlement investments. I told him I wasn't interested. I didn't believe they were legitimate. Later that week, I realized that my answer hadn't been sufficient, and that he might go on to sell the "investments" to other people and those people would be injured even though I might have been in a position to prevent it. I called Adam back and told him that I couldn't participate in that investment. I couldn't find that it made sense. But I wanted to know anybody who had invested and who might be considering investing again. Sure enough, he did know investors and I asked him if he would mind having them come to my office to convince me it was a good investment. He was quite excited.

I presumed he thought he might make a commission but I told

him that I also wanted the opportunity to try to convince his investors not to invest any more, and I wanted to try to persuade him not to sell Scott's settlement "investments" to anyone. I knew Adam was hoping to make a lot of money on this tremendous opportunity, but I knew the opportunity was not real. Adam told me that would be fine.

I said, "Remember, Adam, if I talk you into not pitching the investments or convince your investor not to invest further, you are going to lose business."

He said he was prepared for that possibility. But like any good salesman, he must have been thinking, "Just let me get in front of you and I will sell you."

Adam brought *Sam* to my office. Sam walked into my office all energized with two big folders of paper, hoping to sell me on the confidential settlement investments. Sam had already spent $2,000,000 and a relative of his had invested another $2,000,000 on Rothstein's settlement agreements. He knew others who had spent even more. I didn't know Sam so I tried not to use the words "fraud," "scam," or "Ponzi scheme" when I was talking about the settlement agreements. It was not easy. Instead, I tried to sound confused and naïve, as if I wanted to invest but I just couldn't understand how it all worked. Rather than statements, especially negative ones, I turned each of my twelve red flags into a question. Sam, like any good salesman, tried to show me how it worked, but at the end Sam said, "Alan, this isn't an average investment. It sounds like either this doesn't exist or it is great."

"Sam, those are your words, not mine," I told him. "I think you are right, it's possible it doesn't exist. It even seems probable that it doesn't exist."

By now Sam was quite anxious because he had a lot of money into what he was beginning to think was not real. But he told me that Scott's firm had sent payments on time. I explained that this meant that either the investments were real and Scott would keep sending payments, or they are not real and Scott's firm is doing it just to get more and more people involved before they stop. At that point, I thought I had convinced Sam that the settlements were not real and then he left. He was as panicky as I've ever seen anyone. Adam gave me a call a few minutes later and told me I saved him twenty-five dollars.

I asked, "How?"

He said, "I planned to take Sam to lunch, but Sam was so nervous he couldn't wait to get home to check out his other documents. Actually you saved me thirty dollars, because I was going to buy him dessert as well."

A couple of days went by, and it turned out Sam still had some doubts about what we had discussed. I suggested that Adam and Sam come back to my office but this time bring with them the three settlement agreements that Sam purchased with his relatives. Those agreements represented about $6,000,000 in settlements that were purchased for about $4,000,000. I thought if I saw the settlement agreements there might be further proof that the underlying cases didn't exist. I didn't know exactly what they would show but, since I was so certain this whole situation was a scam, I believed that everything I looked at would offer further proof. Sure enough, Adam and Sam came back, and Sam showed me the three settlement agreements. Each one was ten pages. I thought, *How convenient. The agreements are all going to be the same. How nice it must be when someone comes in to settle a case for more than $3,000,000 and they just wire you the money and they ask, 'Where do I sign?' It doesn't exist in this world.*

I found myself constantly saying to Sam, "It doesn't exist in this world." I'm not even sure if I meant the world as a whole or if I meant the world of law or just the world of labor and employment law. It's not an expression I had ever used before, but I kept finding myself repeating it.

I looked through the agreements quite carefully with Sam and then Sam pointed out there were two differences in the agreements. The first change was that on the older settlement agreement the name was redacted throughout all ten pages. On the two newer agreements, instead of redacting the name on pages two through ten, the name was redacted on page one, and the words "plaintiff" and "defendant" were inserted on page one as defined terms. Throughout the remainder of the document, the terms "plaintiff" and "defendant" appeared rather than names so there was no need to redact them. I suggested that that means the volume of sales of these fabricated documents must have gotten to the point where, for efficiency purposes, Scott needed to do that. It just must have become a nightmare to redact so much information.

Sam suggested maybe it was the same attorney that represented the defendant in each of the three cases. *Fair enough*, I thought. I looked at the paragraph with the name and address of the defense attorney. The name and address were, of course, redacted, but since the agreements were prepared using word processing, where the name and address appeared they took up a different amount of space in each agreement and wrapped the words at the end of the line to the next line. Therefore, we concluded that there were different names and addresses for attorneys in each of the three agreements. Now that we could determine that there were three different defense attorneys, it defied logic that in three different cases involving between just under $1,000,000 to over $3,000,000, attorneys would review agreements and not make any changes in the documents. As I kept saying, "It doesn't exist in this world. It just couldn't be." Even if there is nothing to change, it is the nature of an attorney to want to change something, even if it's merely to let the client see he knows what he's doing or to justify his fee.

We looked at the second change to see if perhaps that would shed some light on the validity of the documents. In the oldest agreement, attorneys' fees were calculated based upon the amount of the settlement. Even though I believed that the agreements were fabricated, once there was a "settlement" amount, calculations had to be made, and if such calculations were not accurate it would surely draw attention and create concern. In the later agreements, I noticed that instead of calculating the legal fees, attorneys' fees were provided for outside of that agreement. Again, this was not proof of the existence of real documents, but instead corroborated my earlier theory that efficiencies were being implemented to make the fraud work smoother and with less effort.

When I looked at the differences, I said, "Sam, those don't prove that a defense attorney made changes. I think those prove that this whole thing is phony."

Sam never gave up. He said, "Maybe Rothstein said to the defendants, 'This is the agreement. Take it or leave it. If you don't sign it, we will file suit.'"

"Not a chance," I said. "The caliber of attorneys handling cases like these would not accept such terms. Even if the defendant's conduct is egregious, there is still a point when there is a line drawn in the sand and the defendant will say, 'Sue me.'" If that was not the case, the amount of every settlement would be even more ridiculously high.

I told Adam and Sam to call up the five biggest law firms in the state and speak to the head of the labor and employment department at each firm.

I said, "Mention that you are considering filing a case for sexual harassment but before you make an appointment you want to know how many sexual harassment cases the firm handles, how many cases the head attorney handles, what the likelihood is of settling a case without filing suit, and how many cases the firm settles annually without filing suit and for what amounts."

I was beyond certain that Adam and Sam could call as many firms as they wanted and they would have a hard time finding any firm that settled five sexual harassment cases per year for a minimum of $500,000 each just by writing a letter. I knew even if that number was wrong, it wouldn't be wrong by much, and I knew it would reach nowhere near the 3,000 cases a year Scottie Rothstein alleged he handled personally.

Then I remembered that Adam's son was an attorney with a national law firm. I suggested that he call his son and brief him on the facts of these cases and ask him if these investments could possibly exist. I mentioned to both Adam and Sam that if Rothstein was really generating over 3,000 cases a year, there must be capable lawyers on the other side. Adam called his son, and he didn't get too far before his son said, "It's impossible, it just doesn't exist. There is not a chance those agreements are real." His son also said, "If they were real, my firm would be defending a number of these cases and it is not." He concluded by stating, "Nobody is defending them because they don't exist."

Sam was happy to meet with me on those two occasions, and based on our conversations he did not invest any further funds. He contacted someone at the group he invested through and alerted them to my concerns. This triggered an immediate trip from New Jersey to Fort Lauderdale by the group's CPA to meet with Scottie Rothstein directly. Fortunately they never mentioned my name and hopefully they didn't even know my name. Interestingly, Scottie produced some financial statements for them to see. No doubt they were doctored financial statements, but they looked real enough to the CPA that he had confidence that the settlement agreements were real. I was told the group then invested $600,000 more.

I didn't understand. I thought it was now obvious that all of these agreements could be doctored and everything could be fabricated. So how could a CPA alerted to the possibility of a scam look at financial statements and accept them as evidence of real agreements? The question confounded me.

Sam asked me if Scott had only sold a few cases, and the names were not redacted, and the return on the investors' money was twenty percent, and the agreements were all different, would that make the agreements legitimate?

"No," I said. "It would just have not raised red flags and it would have been easier to fool me." Fortunately, Sam did not make any further investments with Rothstein.

It occurred to me I now had more pertinent information for the FBI. The lack of meaningful differences in the wording of the three purchased "settlement agreements" created an additional substantial likelihood the agreements were all fabricated. I also had the name and number of another contact who could set an appointment with Rothstein for an FBI agent posing as an investor. In addition, I realized that during my conversation with the FBI, I had never mentioned that I had a business plan detailing Rothstein's program. I thought the FBI might want a copy of it.

On October 2, 2009, I contacted the FBI again to share with the analyst the additional information I had for him. After asking for the analyst with whom I had previously spoken, I was connected to someone's voicemail, and it was not the person I asked for so I hung up. A couple of hours later I called again and said that I had been connected with the wrong person. The operator explained that the initial analyst was no longer the person handling the matter but she would connect me to the proper agent, and if voicemail picked up I should leave a message so the agent could get back to me. Again I reached voicemail. This time I left a message explaining why I was calling and that I had important additional information substantiating what I previously reported. My call was never returned. I waited for a return call until October 14, and then I again called the FBI and again left a message. The call was never returned. I began to understand completely how the whistleblower in the Madoff matter felt when he reported the matter to the SEC and the agency showed little interest.

Frustrated, I again reviewed my options. The only one that seemed like a possibility was calling the attorney general and speaking with him directly if he would take my call. I was not yet ready to take that risk. I also was not convinced it was my responsibility to make inquires of RRA's employment law attorneys as to the volume of their work. If my second voicemail was not soon returned, I was going to go to the FBI office in person since they already had my name.

Growing impatient, I called a friend of mine who worked for RRA in a satellite office, and told him I needed to speak with him outside of his office and I asked him if he could go downstairs and call me on his cell phone. I asked my friend if either his firm or Scott Rothstein was selling settlement agreements on cases the firm generated and settled without filing suit. He told me not to his knowledge, but he would find out.

I cautioned him not to use my name and not to speak to anyone who might relay the information to Scott Rothstein. He assured me my name would not be repeated. I told him that he couldn't even repeat my name to his closest confidant in the firm, but I did tell him I didn't trust Scott Rothstein at all, and advised him not to put any money in the firm's trust account. I said that I didn't have any actual proof of any wrongdoing but I just didn't trust Scottie and since it was so easy anyway to put money in the opposing counsel's trust accounts, I asked him to do that. He agreed. I wouldn't let him ask questions because I didn't want him to know too much, and then get scared and slip up, possibly telling someone who would get word back to Scott.

He called me back a couple of days later and reported that a person close to Scottie confirmed that Scottie was selling settlement agreements. They were not RRA settlements but he had set up a national clearinghouse for selling settlements. To me, it was further proof the agreements did not exist since Scott had said all settlement proceeds were wired directly into RRA's trust account. If other firms settled the cases the money would not go directly into RRA's account. Also, this was the first time anyone had even suggested that not all the settlements were coming out of RRA. Scott himself had told me that he was personally settling these cases. How could he if these cases didn't even belong to his firm? It was clear Scott was lying to his own attorneys. This was another inconsistency the FBI needed to be told. I vowed to continue doing what I could to bring down Rothstein, yet events were about to supersede my efforts.

In my community, kindnesses are done quietly and without fanfare. This is quite the opposite of Rothstein's world where every purported kindness and act of charity is publicized to the fullest extent possible. Here is one fine example of such discretion and selflessness.

The Big Move

Penina and Shalom Grossman were making the big move. Though they lived in a small town in the Northeast and enjoyed the comforts of a large house, they had signed a lease for a two-bedroom apartment in North Miami Beach. When they got back home and began to pack, they were unsure just how many of their home furnishings would fit in their new abode. If only they had taken measurements of the new place, they would have had a better idea. Then they realized they needed to be sure that the electricity and water would be on when they arrived as the landlord had promised.

Penina Grossman called Raquel Knobel, one of the few people she knew in North Miami Beach, and asked if she could impose on her to check and make sure the water and electricity were turned on and, if not, to make arrangements for both utilities to be on. After Raquel agreed, Penina asked if it was too much to ask for another favor, to take some measurements. Raquel was only too happy to help out. She was actually thrilled to receive the call because it got her just what she wanted: access to the Grossmans' apartment before they moved in. Raquel obtained the key from the Grossmans' new landlord, confirmed the water and electricity were on, and then took the measurements as requested and some photographs as well. The Grossmans were very appreciative of Raquel's kindness, but had no idea just how kind Raquel was.

Raquel knew that the Grossmans' last move had not been a happy one and that they were very uncomfortable in their present community. She was determined to make sure the move to North Miami Beach did not resemble their last move. The Knobels met Penina on the first trip she had made to North Miami Beach a couple of years earlier to investigate the community. It was Penina's *Shabbos* meals with the Knobels that convinced her that North Miami Beach was where her family belonged. In particular, Penina was attracted to the North Miami Beach's community's tolerance of all different levels of Jewish religiosity, as the Grossmans were relatively new to the world of Orthodoxy. A year later the entire Grossman family visited the community and a combination of *Shabbos* meals with the Knobels and another family to whom the Knobels introduced them sealed their decision to move.

Just before the time for the Grossmans' arrival, Raquel asked the landlord for the key to their apartment once again. Raquel and her daughter, Shaina, put up welcome signs throughout the apartment, stocked the apartment with basic paper goods and cleansers, and filled the refrigerator with some groceries. They also placed a flower arrangement on the kitchen counter so when the Grossmans picked up the keys and walked in, they would know from the start they were in the right community. Raquel put together the traditional "move into a new home good-luck package" which included candles, a bottle of olive oil, a box of matza, a container of water, and a container of salt. Needless to say, the Grossman family felt *very* welcomed upon their arrival, and despite their exhaustion, were extremely grateful to have a fresh start and to feel welcomed in their new home.

Compared with Scott's huge public donations to various Fort Lauderdale charities, Raquel's simple gesture of providing ordinary basics to a family who is new in town might seem insignificant. However, Raquel's actions were sincere and heartfelt with no obvious benefit to the giver except the knowledge that she had made another family happy.

Chapter 11

The Firm Implodes

*If your actions inspire others
to dream more, learn more, do more
and become more, you are a leader.*

—JOHN QUINCY ADAMS

T ABOUT SIX P.M. on Sunday, November 1, 2009, my cell phone vibrated two or three times, but I was in the middle of the evening services so I didn't look at my phone. As I walked out of *shul*, I saw that I had missed a few calls. Because a friend had called at least a couple of times and he generally didn't call on Sundays, I thought the calls must have been important. Moshe had also called to ask if something happened to RRA. I said I didn't know, I hadn't heard anything at all, but I was about to find out.

I made a call to a friend and asked if anything had happened at the firm. I was told it imploded; nobody knew what had happened, but all the money was gone. Scott Rothstein was out of the country and no one was sure where. Nobody seemed to know anything but the whole office was swarming with FBI agents and IRS agents.

A great weight had lifted from my shoulders, and I thought to myself, what a relief for me! I could actually walk outside and not look over my shoulder, worried that Scottie might see me as a threat to his scheme. I envisioned that at that moment he did not have a friend in the world. I thought every politician would soon be disavowing any relationship with him. Charities would be announcing they didn't know who he was. Entertainers and athletes would be saying he wasn't really their friend. Law enforcement personnel would be saying they never gave him special treatment. He would even be removed from the inner circle of the governor, taken off the Judicial Nominating Committee of the Fourth Judicial District and removed from the Sheriff's Advisory Council. My guess was that within minutes, the Florida Bar Association would announce that his license to practice law was suspended or revoked. As far as his mode of dress, he would soon be fitted for a pin-striped outfit that didn't look anything like his custom-tailored Italian designer suits. His transportation would be in the backseat of a standard police car rather than his usual fancy, showy car. His expensive cigars, martinis, bottles of wine, and meals at Bova Prime would come to a sudden and permanent halt.

Two weeks before the RRA implosion, I had visited my doctor for a routine exam. My doctor was concerned with my blood pressure and, for the first time ever, not only increased my blood pressure medication, but doubled it. The day after the implosion, I doubted that I needed the double dose any longer, so the next morning I cut the dose to what it had been. A few weeks later I dropped by the doctor's office and found my blood pressure was normal again.

In many ways, Scott Rothstein was like a balloon. His "friends," business associates, partners, charitable institutions, politicians, sports figures, entertainers, and others were like helium for him. They helped him rise and grow bigger. But one small poke with a pin and there was nothing left of Rothstein. Once Scott had fled the country, everyone quickly started backpedaling and tried to point out, retroactively, how they had disassociated themselves with him, but had they? Take, for instance, political trickster Roger Stone.

On November 4, 2009, Roger wrote on his blog, *StoneZone*:

"Rothstein's spending became so profligate that one year ago I retained Adam Mangino, a former DEA agent, to investigate and determine the source of Rothstein's newfound wealth. While Mangino could not determine the source of Rothstein's wild spending, he did advise me that the money was not Rothstein's.

I asked Rothstein to dissolve RRA Consulting LLC a year ago and his sponsorship of the StoneZone ended July 29th of this year. I am not an investor in any of his schemes and can't believe anyone in their right mind would entrust him with investor money."

Stone even wrote, "… Rothstein always seemed to me to be more interested in the 'appearance' of success and influence rather than the reality of either."

But that is not what Stone had written about Rothstein in his blog just two months earlier, on August 27, 2009. At that time in his article entitled "Florida's Next Senator," Stone's suggestion to Governor Crist on filling the Senate seat being vacated by Mel Martinez was "… why not appoint some one [sic] with no clients in Tallahassee?"

"Fort Lauderdale Lawyer Scott Rothstein has a distinguished legal record, has been a key supporter of Governor Crist and John McCain, has un [sic] unmatched record of philanthropic activities and would bring an unconventional style of getting things done to Washington. Add Rothstein to the short list."

Interesting! Appoint Rothstein Senator. I like it. Yes, he would have been the perfect candidate. Stone says, "he [Rothstein] would bring an unconventional style of getting things done to Washington."

I bet he would. But didn't Stone mention he could not "believe anyone in their right mind would entrust him with investor money [?]" Yet less than two months earlier he was willing to recommend Rothstein for managing taxpayer money! Why? Can you imagine Rothstein as a U.S. senator? Of course, in some ways he would fit right in. He would be able to wheel and deal from the get-go with no learning curve needed. But what committee would he be appointed to? Oh, yes, the Senate Committee on Social Security and the Committee on Campaign Reform. I suggest those committees since thinking about Rothstein's Ponzi scheme got me thinking about well-intentioned government programs that are not on sound financial ground. The first one that came to mind was Social Security, which, though intended for the good of the country, is, as it stands now, headed for financial disaster. The same is true with campaign financing; it is a dismal failure. The prohibition of insider trading is also well-intended when it comes to the average person, but Congress left a gaping hole when it came to permitting its members to trade on privileged information.

Our leaders should lead by example. It is time that our leaders stop doing things just because they can. If Social Security is so great, why don't congressmen contribute to Social Security? I will tell you why. They know better. They have a real retirement plan. For themselves they will not contribute to an unsound program like Social Security. So why is it a requirement for us?

According to the government's official Social Security web site, ssa.gov, when The Social Security Act was signed into law in 1935, the Social Security tax was two percent of the first $3,000 of an employee's income. One half of the tax was paid by the employer and one half by the employee. By 1950 the tax rate was increased to three percent and over time gradually increased to 12.40 percent. All the while, the maximum portion of wages the tax was payable on also increased. As it increased, it remained one half the burden of the employee and one half the responsibility of the employer. According to the 2007 OASDI (Old-Age, Survivors, and Disability Insurance program) Trustees Report, the Trustees recommend increasing the Social Security tax rate to 16.41 percent in 2041 and 17.60 percent in 2081 or cutting benefits by twenty-five percent in 2041 and by an additional five percent in 2081. Keep in mind that this is in addition to the Medicaid tax, which is already rising, federal income taxes and in many areas, state and local income taxes and property taxes.

In 1983 up to fifty percent of the Social Security benefits received became subject to taxation. In 1993 the amount increased to eighty-five percent. In 1950, 13.8 percent of the population was receiving

Social Security. Intermediate projections showed that in 2010, twenty-one percent of the population of this country will be receiving Social Security and by 2035, that percentage will skyrocket to thirty-six percent. The picture is clear: future generations will continue to pay more to receive less or nothing at all if it implodes. All the while, the first ones in the system receive payments from the next ones in. As long as the population and dollars keep growing, everything is fine. Once that stops, the party is over.

Social Security, like Rothstein's Ponzi scheme, paid the first contributors much more than they contributed. Ida May Fuller was the first monthly recipient of Social Security. She paid in $24.75 and her employer paid the same on her three year's income of $2,475; she received $22,888.92 over the next thirty-five years of her life. Not bad – she received back 462 times what she and her employer contributed. It sounds like Rothstein's numbers. No, it's better than Rothstein, it's about 1,220 percent per year (An average of $653.96 per year on a contribution of $49.50 after retirement). As the population increases more slowly and a higher proportion of the country is older and living longer, mathematically speaking, we end up with a Rothstein-esque problem. Like Rothstein, the government can print more paper. But can our country sustain a 17.60 percent Social Security tax and higher Medicaid taxes, federal income taxes and state and local taxes?

Social Security is not the only sad example of a well-intentioned but fundamentally unsound program operated by the government. Let us consider "insider trading." Insider trading is the illegal buying and selling of securities by persons acting on privileged information. You and I will go to jail if we do it, and many Americans have gone to jail for insider trading. But congressmen have privileged information they are permitted to trade on and it is legal. Congressmen are able to trade on political intelligence that they learn in committees that is not yet available to the public. They also can make legislative decisions that have a direct impact on stocks they own. Representatives Baird and Slaughter have introduced legislation to require disclosure of such trades and prohibit profiteering on political intelligence that has not yet been disseminated to the public in the same manner as insider trading. Bud W. Jerke[5] argues that it should not be treated as insider trading but as political corruption. Jerke argues that treating it as insider information would only stop the trading on nonpublic information, it would not stop the voting based upon "maximizing existing portfolios." Treating it as insider trading would also hamper the early dissemination and evaluation of the information which would, he argues be a disservice to the public.

It's time our leaders lead by example and not carve out special exceptions for themselves. It is important for Congress to either pass the Stop Trading on Congressional Knowledge Act (STOCK Act) which will prohibit members of Congress and their staff from using nonpublic information they are able to obtain through their official positions to enrich their personal portfolios or to treat the profiteering by them on the nonpublic information as political corruption. One has to wonder why, if legislators find it so offensive for Wall Street executives to trade on confidential information, members of Congress have resisted passing a law requiring them to disclose their stock transactions within ninety days of trades and to stop trading on confidential information.

What about campaign contributions? Did Rothstein make a mockery of the system? Absolutely. But he was in good company. The politicians got real cozy with Scott and grabbed his money as fast as he handed it out. Maybe someone can explain to me why individuals are limited with respect to the amount they can give a candidate, but a slush fund indirectly benefiting the candidate can be created in the form of an Electioneering Communication Organization, a Political Action Committee, or a Party and then it is a free-for-all. There is no limit on contributions. I did not know how it worked until Rothstein explained it by demonstration. Maybe Scott was a little brazen with his approach but maybe that is what we needed in order to understand how ridiculous the system is in its current form.

5 Cashing in on Capitol Hill: Insider Trading and the Use of Political Intelligence for Profit, University of Pennsylvania Law Review April, 2010, Vol. 15, Issue Number 5, pp. 1451–1521.

When I met with Rothstein, he made a point of mentioning how he had the politicians and law enforcement people in his back pocket. Envision the picture of Governor Crist that hung on Rothstein's wall with the words "Scott – you are amazing!" signed "Charlie Crist." Then visualize the picture of Scott blowing out the candles on the governor's cake for which Rothstein paid Crist $52,000. You might say, "Those are only pictures." And they are. But what happens when the pictures are added to the amounts and timing of checks. Then what does it look like?

On November 18, 2009, journalist Buddy Nevins wrote on *Browardbeat.com* the following:

> "On January 26, 2009, Rothstein and his law firm Rothstein Rosenfeldt Adler gave $100,000 to the RPOF [Republican Party of Florida]. Two days later, Judges Carlos Rodriguez and Barbara McCarthy were appointed by Crist."

> "On July 28, 2008, Rothstein's firm gave $52,000 to the RPOF. That was the same day that Jay Hurley was appointed to the county court. One day later, Rothstein's firm donated another $25,000 to the RPOF."

On December 1, 2009, "The Buzz," a *St. Petersburg Times* blog, reported that, "[Governor] Crist appointed Rothstein to the 4th DCA [District Court of Appeals] Judicial nominating commission on August 25, 2008, four days before Rothstein contributed $140,000 to the RPOF [Republican Party of Florida]." Democratic U. S. Senate candidate Maurice Ferre had demanded an investigation to see if the governor was trading judicial appointments for money. Rothstein chose the timing for the political contributions, not the governor. But why would the governor allow anyone to make things look the way they looked? Our leaders need to be able to say, "No, it is not right," and then turn down money. A leader must not only *be* honest but a leader must appear honest, take responsibility, have discipline, and have a vision of something other than being elected and re-elected. A leader sets the tone. More than one hundred years ago, James Freeman Clarke said, "A politician thinks of the next election - a statesman of the next generation." Those words remain true.

Stone and Crist weren't the only ones who quickly worked hard to distance themselves from Rothstein. According to Sydney P. Freedberg's article on December 29, 2009, in the *St. Petersburg Times*, on August 27, 2009, Alex Sink and the Democratic Party raised $243,000 at Rothstein's home, primarily for the campaign of Alex Sink, democratic candidate for governor of Florida. Yet Sink, who is Florida's chief financial officer, said about 100 people were there and that she barely interacted with her host. "I maybe spoke with [Rothstein] for two minutes," she said. Quite amazing, really. Freedburg wrote that about a month later:

> "Rothstein's firm landed on a list of law firms being considered for potentially lucrative work with the State Board of Administration – with an assist from Sink's chief of staff. Sink, who along with Gov. Charlie Crist and Attorney General Bill McCollum oversee the board, said there was no connection between the contribution and her deputy's intervention for Rothstein's firm. She said she didn't know her chief of staff had put in a word for the law firm until the *St. Petersburg Times* asked her about it …. Critics question how Rothstein's firm, with little experience in the securities field, got on the list of invitees to compete for complex, taxpayer-funded legal work …. For the law firms, the work could mean tens of millions in fees. Looking for an edge, more than four dozen firms spent hundreds of thousands on Florida politics, hiring lobbyists and contributing to political groups and politicians."

In mid-November 2009, a couple of weeks after Scott's downfall, I attended a wedding and an acquaintance came over and thanked me for saving his $150,000. He explained that his attorney did not deposit the $150,000 he gave him for a real estate transaction into RRA's trust account based upon my request. He said but for my request, he would have lost his money.

And then there was this response from an acquaintance, Albert. Albert called me after reading in the newspaper that I turned Rothstein in to the FBI and he had this to say: "Alan, I was so appreciative that when you knew I was trying to line up investors for Rothstein's settlement business, you spent hours convincing me it was a scam and to keep far away. I went to sleep that night grateful that I knew you. I believed you saved my reputation and spared me endless grief. I am embarrassed to say that when I woke up in the morning, my thoughts were different. In the morning I was thinking, what a nut I am, not to bring in investors. This is an opportunity of a lifetime to make endless money, I thought. Why would I possibly give up such an opportunity? I would explain to the investors that it was worth looking into. It is with a prominent law firm and the CEO is a close friend of Governor Crist and law enforcement. I would explain also that some people think it is too good to be true. I would leave it to the investor to decide."

He had investors lined up to meet with Rothstein but fortunately the operation imploded before his meeting with Rothstein and before any of his investors invested. He told me that looking back he was just overwhelmed by greed!

There is an absence of leadership when so much money is flowing. Fort Lauderdale Police Chief Adderley stated that "he didn't suspect Rothstein [of criminal activity.] ... But Adderley also pointed out he was not the only public figure who had a relationship with Rothstein." He took no responsibility for his conduct. He refused to be held accountable. "I can't be ashamed," Adderley said, "because I'm not the only one."

I guess the expressions popularized by President Harry S. Truman, "The buck stops here" and "If you can't stand the heat, get out of the kitchen" don't apply to a great many of our political leaders. We need that mentality back. We need campaign reform that will allow candidates to run for office without needing to raise so much money from the public that there is the expectation of a return on the investment. The system in place today makes it difficult for any honest person to want to run for public office. Candidates for major political offices need so much money to win re-election that, from the day they are elected, they are raising money to get re-elected. They literally become addicted to money and like all addicts they do whatever it takes to feed their habit. That explains why many "leaders" vote on bills the way they do. Rather than listen to what they say, the very best way to understand politicians' voting patterns is to view which PACs, ECOs, and parties contribute heavily to their campaigns or make expenditures that benefit them. Rothstein fed addicted politicians money and he certainly seemed to get their attention.

What is especially disturbing with regard to campaign contributions is the Supreme Court's 5-4 decision in <u>Citizens United v. Federal Election Commission</u>, that was decided on January 21, 2010. In that decision, the Court overruled two important precedents about the First Amendment rights of corporations and decided that the government may not ban political spending by corporations in candidate elections. Although the case involved a media corporation, the majority opinion held that as a practical matter, it is difficult to distinguish between media corporations and other types of corporations. The impassioned dissent, authored by Justice John Paul Stevens, argues that the Court made a grave error in treating corporate speech the same as speech by human beings.

Justice Stevens wrote, "The difference between selling a vote and selling access is a matter of degree, not kind. And selling access is not qualitatively different from giving special preference to those who spent money on one's behalf."

In 1989, Allen Pross, the executive director of the California Medical Association's PAC said, "We don't buy votes. What we do is we buy a candidate's stance on an issue."

I'd love it if he could explain the difference to me. I'd love it even more if I could keep a straight face while he was doing the explaining.

The real-life effect of the decision is that it seems that, although individuals are limited in the amount of campaign contributions they can make, all one needs to do is form a corporation and spend the money in a manner that will benefit his candidacy and there is no limit to the amount of money that a corporation can spend. Now corporations can, as Allen Pross said, "buy a candidate's stance on an issue."

In a statement shortly after the decision, President Obama called it "a green light to a new stampede of special interest money in our politics." Two leading Democrats, Senator Charles E. Schumer of New York and Representative Chris Van Hollen of Maryland, said that they had been working for months to draft legislation in response to the anticipated decision.

We need real campaign finance reform with meaningful limits on the amounts of contributions possible, including contributions to PACs, ECOs, parties and corporations. Part and parcel of reform is to recognize that there is little difference between giving a candidate a $100,000 contribution and spending $100,000 on his behalf. The candidate understands that if his position on issues differs from the spender's, the spending will stop. If limits are in place, then for every dollar raised up to the limit, taxpayer money should be contributed as matching funds. The matching funds may be 3-1, or 4-1 or whatever it takes so the taxpayers own the elected officials again and leaders can spend their time working for the public rather than for re-election.

Throughout our daily lives we see the effects of our distrust of authorities and organizations that were once considered beyond reproach. When buyers of securities do not trust our rating agencies, a higher spread results between the yield on U.S. Treasury Bonds and what investments are priced at in the marketplace, even for those investments we once considered "safe." We consequently will pay more to get less. Rothstein has brought us further down that same path. If we do not say "enough" and change direction, the cost of doing business will continue to go up since no one will trust any document or any person. Nations remain great when leaders lead by example and citizens demand more of themselves as a result. Look at the number of employees or spouses of employees at RRA that gave between $50,000 and $450,000 in political contributions in one year and received bonuses for nearly the same amounts at about the time they made the contributions. Hello! Did the candidates really believe those large checks had anything to do with what the candidates would do for the country, rather than what they would do *to* our country?

America is the greatest country in the world. To remain great, we need to be leaders and look like leaders to the world and especially to ourselves. Douglas Adams said it best when he said, "To give real service you must add something which cannot be bought or measured with money, and that is sincerity and integrity."

This is what we must demand of our leaders and so we must adjust our system to make this more possible. Political leaders can govern with their hearts on the right side. They need only ask the question, "What is best for America?" instead of, "What is best for me or my campaign contributors?" Simply changing the question that is asked will change America immensely.

Folks, we can do better and we will if we demand it of ourselves and our leaders. Let's start today because people are important; together we will make a difference.

I tell these stories not to puff myself up, but to speak to what it is like to live in a culture and community where people look out for each other, not for their own selfish interests and immediate gratification. With that notion in mind, here's a story about kindness and consideration for others.

Helping The Sick

About seven years ago, I went to see someone in a nursing home. As I went down the hall toward the patient's room, I noticed my neighbor *Chaim's* name on a door. After my visit, I stopped by Chaim's room to say, "Hello." Chaim and his dear wife moved to our community from the Northeast a couple of years or so before this incident. Due to his worsening health and immobility, Chaim did not make it to *shul* or other community events and as a result was relatively invisible. I had noticed his absence and was pleased to have a few minutes to spend with him.

As I knocked lightly on the door, the door began to open. Chaim invited me in. After a few minutes, Chaim said, "You probably are wondering why I am so cheerful. I do not think you ever saw me in such a good mood."

Before I could answer, Chaim asked, "Do you have time to listen to a story?"

I said, "Sure," and he shared a beautiful story with me.

Chaim told me that his wife was taken to the hospital a few weeks earlier and he was home alone. His wife knew that he was in no condition to care for himself so she called *Bikur Cholim* (Hebrew for helping the sick) of North Miami Beach and asked if someone would provide him with dinner and wash his clothes. Two volunteers arrived from *Bikur Cholim* immediately to assure him that they would provide meals and tend to his clothes while his wife was in the hospital. During that visit, the *Bikur Cholim* volunteers told Chaim that after observing him and speaking with him, they believed he needed to be in a nursing home with skilled care. The ladies were concerned that he was too ill to be at home. Chaim was still recovering from a recent serious ailment that left him in need of therapy.

Chaim did not disagree. He did tell the two women that a nursing home was not an option since he did not have the funds, insurance, or government benefits to pay for it. They would not hear of it. They said all that was important was determining what was needed and then they would do everything they could to be sure it was provided. After serving him a beautiful meal and providing him with clean clothes, they had him transported to the nursing home where I visited him. This was possible once they explained the circumstances to a neighbor who was the administrator of the nursing home. They informed him of the dire need and asked for help while they tried to sort out if, and how, the nursing home could be paid. The women were going to see if Chaim qualified for Medicaid or Social Security Disability but they wanted to be sure he was cared for in the interim.

Chaim told me that he had never been treated so beautifully. Other than his wife, he did not have anyone, since his son did not speak to him. With his wife in the hospital and later a convalescent home, he had no one to whom he could turn. Chaim said he was treated like a king. He said that the two ladies from *Bikur Cholim* had families, careers, and plenty of other responsibilities, but they made him feel as if he was all that mattered.

Chaim said, "I may not have my health or contact with my son, but I sure feel like a person again." He felt cared for and that he was important. It was true that I had never seen him so happy before.

About three months later, Chaim passed away. I do not know if the nursing home was ever paid, and if so, by whom. What I do know is that Chaim lived the last few months of his life happy and with dignity because of the way *Bikur Cholim* responded to him. He was an important person, and how he was cared for mattered.

Before I left on the day I visited him, I asked Chaim, "Who were these tremendous people that gave you such care?" and he told me, "Eddie Bursztyn was the nursing home administrator and *Esther Levy* and *Sarah Weiss* were the two *Bikur Cholim* volunteers."

Having individuals like Eddie, Esther and Sarah in our community and an organization like *Bikur Cholim* is part of what makes our community so special because each of them recognizes the importance of acknowledging the dignity of each person and is willing to do what it takes to ensure that each individual receives the type of care required.

Chapter 12

Blessing our Children

If you don't set a baseline standard for what you'll accept in life, you'll find it's easy to slip into behaviors and attitudes or a quality of life that's far below what you deserve.

~ANTHONY ROBBINS

EVERY FRIDAY EVENING as we usher in *Shabbos*, I return home from *shul* and after my family sings a beautiful song together at the table as part of welcoming the *Shabbos*, I put my hands on each child's head from oldest to youngest and give him or her two blessings. The first blessing taken from the *Torah* is a traditional blessing given to children in Jewish homes. The second blessing is my unique custom but is one which my family loves and views now as an integral part of our Friday night ritual.

My wife says that she knows how my week went or what went on during my week by listening carefully to the second blessing I give. Each week I try to think of a lesson I want to impart to our children and I incorporate it in my blessing. Oftentimes it is something I observed during the week that went well or something I noticed that needed work, or it's something they need to stay away from or protect themselves against or guard against. On other occasions I tailor the second blessing to something specific about each of our children. It may be a position they received in school or in the community or it could be something they are trying to accomplish or something they need to work extra hard to achieve.

In the past I had all day on Friday to think about what that blessing would be. For the last five years we have had at least one of our children in school in Israel and for one year we had two children there. With the clock seven hours ahead in Israel, by nine in the morning (our time) on Friday, I needed to have prepared my blessing to give to my children in Israel.

The week of November 7, 2009, I knew I had to make sense of what happened with the Scottie Rothstein situation and come away with a message to communicate to our children. I knew what happened and I knew that one should stay as far away from dishonesty as possible. I knew the dangers of being greedy, but I hadn't fully digested just what happened and how I was able to walk out of this nightmare the same person as the one who walked in. But that's what I needed to understand so I could help protect our children from ever getting close to the same dreadful situation.

Living within one's means, in fact, even living below one's means, would be a good message, but it wasn't the message that summed up all I saw. Appearance alone without substance is shallow and meaningless is also an important truth but that too didn't sum up all I had witnessed. Be a person who lives with your heart on the right side was another great message, but that was always a great message. This situation only highlighted it.

I also thought about the importance of avoiding getting involved even in small acts that are dishonest or could lead to dishonesty, because one minor thing leads to another and a person hardly notices the difference. Soon a person can become involved in something extremely dishonest or shockingly indecent without even realizing he is doing anything wrong. All true, but I wanted to give a message of how to avoid finding oneself in an inappropriate situation, not just to avoid it. I then realized that I needed to look at what it was in my life that helped me notice such a sharp contrast between right and wrong, between truth and falsehood, between a way I want to live and a way I want to avoid living.

What grounds me are the influences from my wife, my parents, my community, and my friends. My wife and I share a value system and she is very insightful and wise. Thankfully, Leah is not "high maintenance." For instance, I was never a morning person and I was always used to sleeping just a few extra minutes. I would sleep a little later and pray by myself at home at least until I saw just how much my wife enjoyed knowing that I got up earlier and prayed with a *minyan* (quorum of ten males for communal prayer) at *shul* each morning. Consequently, one of the reasons I went to *shul* each morning was because I knew this made Leah happy. And thanks to Leah, I also came to see how powerful praying with a *minyan* is to start off each day when expressing gratitude to G-d for everything I have and to ask G-d every morning for everything I need. It has made me a stronger person, although it's still not easy. My wife values the time I spend during the day, each day, to learn the *Torah*. Leah would rather that I take off a little time from work and spend more time on spiritual pursuits. Because Leah does not desire a fancy house, car, or other material objects, she is happy living within our means and prefers using our resources to help others.

My second great influence is our community. We are fortunate to live in an Orthodox Jewish community in North Miami Beach, Florida, where our neighbors do unbelievable acts of kindness for each other, not just on occasion, but constantly. This inspires me immensely. The people and the infrastructure of our community help ground me with what's right and to recognize something that's wrong.

The third great influence in my life is having great role models. I was fortunate to grow up in a home where I saw that a life well lived was measured by helping other people, not by accumulating possessions.

Friends are a fourth great influence in my life. I try and make sure to surround myself with friends who are good people. To a great extent people are influenced by the people around them. It's harder to grow when one is around people who drag one down so friends are a very important part of our life. One must learn to surround oneself with people who inspire him to be a better person.

As I think about it, there is even a fifth great influence in my life – our children, our children's friends, and the schools our children attend. Our home, much like the home I grew up in, is always filled with our children's friends. Sometimes our house seems like Grand Central Station and we love it. Our children make sure to involve themselves in activities that help other people, whether it's visiting nursing homes (and sometimes even dressing up as clowns to visit nursing homes), visiting neighbors who are ill or physically handicapped, or mentoring children who attend public school. Our children also get involved with taking charge of projects, whether it's being in charge of matching students with neighbors who need a little extra help or being in charge of a school project or play or any other worthwhile activity.

With all those deliberations in mind, the Friday after RRA collapsed, by the time I was on the way to work, I had solidified my blessing for our children, knowing I would hear early from Israel. Sure enough, just before nine A.M. the phone rang and it was Shira. This time my blessing included just how imperative it is to be grounded and how important it is to select a spouse, role models, a community, and friends, and to make sure that one's children's friends and schools are appropriate. But it also included the need to appreciate that it is imminently easier to avoid temptation than to overcome it. Therefore it is essential to keep far away from inappropriate situations. The *Torah* itself makes it the obligation of our sages to enact safeguards around the *Torah*. We have to take extra precautions not to even come close to violating a *Torah* command. This is to avoid putting a person into a situation where he could easily lose control and fall victim. If ever a situation amplified the need to take precautions to avoid temptations it is Rothstein and Rothstein-like situations.

A person doesn't wake up one morning and decide to destroy his friends, his business associates, his clients, his community, and in many respects the fabric of society, not to mention himself. It's a slow process.

Having low self-esteem, being exceedingly greedy, not having the tools to maturely solve problems, refusing to take personal responsibility, and living with one's heart on the left side for a long period of time all help create the problem. When a person is envious of what another person has, in time that envy will destroy him and will keep him from ever really being happy. A person has only so many birthdays, weddings, graduations, and other monumental occasions in his immediate family. If a person always needs to be the center of attention, most of the time he will be unhappy. If, on the other hand, a person can learn to be happy for the joyous occasions and successes of others, he will always find a reason to be happy. It is an attitude by choice and although not easy for some people, it is worth working on oneself to achieve it since enjoying the successes of others is the only way to truly be a successful person.

Unfortunately, when we become involved in a situation that is intriguing and perhaps a little improper, we might not say anything. We behave like this especially if we are not directly involved. If we are directly involved, and the benefits are tremendous, and any irregularities are minor, soon we become accustomed to ignoring improper conduct. We then go on to build up more and more acceptance to irregularities without even realizing it until it becomes fatal. Our goal needs to be to not accept any conduct that is inappropriate as soon as it starts. If we are not sure, we need to investigate and err on the side of caution. We cannot put ourselves in a situation in which we become tolerant of the intolerable. Our political leaders and law enforcement officers surely need to distance themselves from such conduct rather than stand guard and allow it to occur under their noses.

Unlike Rothstein and his cronies, people in my community respect and revere the law, and use it as an instrument for good, which includes those in need who do not have the resources to pay for the legal services they need. A great example of such a commitment to equal access and selflessness is my neighbor, Moshe Lehrfield.

A Lawyer Committed To Community

Moshe Lehrfield is an attorney and a shareholder of Greenberg Traurig, Florida's second largest law firm and the country's eighth largest with 1,775 lawyers. Unlike Rothstein who displays the written *Torah* as a prop on his desk and gives back to his community with stolen money, Moshe learns and lives the *Torah* and gives back to the community with his time and money.

Rothstein was preoccupied with money, but not Lehrfield. Lehrfield is probably the last one to show up to work but for good reason. He spends the first three hours after morning prayer services learning *Torah*. After a long day at work he returns to learning *Torah*. Between his *Torah* learning, Moshe works hard to serve his clients but among his clients are many community organizations. When Toras Emes and Yeshiva Toras Chaim, two of the schools in our neighborhood, bought their campuses, refinanced their campuses, sold their former school site, suffered hurricane damage, sought zoning changes to expand their campuses and/or need legal assistance in connection with a myriad of other legal matters requiring a skilled and caring attorney, Moshe Lehrfield was and is there for them.

In an average year, Moshe Lehrfield spends approximately 150 hours providing pro bono legal work. For a couple of years when the needs of the community organizations were greater, he spent as much as 400 hours a year on pro bono legal work. Since Moshe's remuneration is based upon billable hours and not just hours worked, the difference between Rothstein and Lehrfield is most apparent. From Moshe's actions, we see that not every attorney is like Rothstein – just chasing dollars and unwilling to give of his skills to help others.

Rothstein's conduct as an attorney became very visible. Now, we need to show the other side, the better side. We need to practice law the way my father used to, when every person was important and when the opportunity to practice law was a sacred privilege to serve. We, as attorneys, need to make a difference. We also need to be more careful in how we practice, how we bill and how we communicate with clients so that the public begins to rank our profession higher than used car salesmen and politicians. We should scrupulously calculate our billable hours and always consider over-producing when our hours say one thing and our results say another. We can no longer do just a good job; our performance now needs to be our best. And we never had a right to bill hours when the cost was not reasonably calculated to be in the client's best interest. We need to regain our profession's reputation. To achieve that, we need to provide services in a manner that will cause a client to be impressed enough to thank us, praise us or recommend us.

Chapter 13

A Sheriff's Escort

*Minds are like parachutes – they only
function when open.*

~Thomas Dewar

S COTT ROTHSTEIN LEFT TOWN on October 27,
2009, for, of all places, Morocco. But this was no spot deci-
sion. But by the same token, it was not planned months in
advance as one would expect of a fraudster involved in a
scheme that has no way out. About ten days before disappearing, he
had sent an email to the attorneys at his office, mentioning that
he had a client that may need to go to a location that does not have
an extradition treaty with the U.S. or Israel. One of the suggestions
he had received was Morocco. That sparked rumors that he might be
there. Word came quickly that attorney Marc Nurik, an attorney for
RRA, was asked to resign from the firm so that he could personally
represent Scott Rothstein.

From media reports, there were many friends, members of his
firm, and true believers in him who seemed totally astonished. The
other half of Broward County claimed they knew something was
wrong but they just didn't know what it was; to them it was no
surprise at all. Scottie had been spending far beyond his means and
far too ostentatiously. On November 3, 2009, Sally Kestin, John
Burstein, and Brittany Wallman of the *Fort Lauderdale Sun-Sentinel*

newspaper quoted Rothstein's only equity partner in the law firm, Stuart Rosenfeldt, as saying that over the years Rothstein had lied to him, but Rosenfeldt added, "The kinds of small lies I caught him in were nothing to lead you to conclude your partner was running a giant scam out of your law firm."

Who could ever have imagined that anyone would ever do something like this? Little things make a difference but when you connect the dots you see how little things add up one after the next. The *Sun-Sentinel* article concluded with these two sentences: "A distraught Rosenfeldt said Monday he feared that Rothstein had destroyed the firm's reputation. 'I think we are going to go down in history in the same way as [Bernie] Madoff, he said.'"

This clearly was an understatement. By Monday morning the law firm had hired a former U.S. Attorney for the Southern District of Florida, Kendall Coffey, to file a suit wrestling control of RRA away from Scott Rothstein to Stuart Rosenfeldt, his co-founder. The attorneys of RRA sought to have a receiver appointed with the objective of saving the firm.

The motion to appoint a receiver stated:

It is with surprise and sorrow that the attorneys of Rothstein Rosenfeldt Adler, P.A. have learned that Scott W. Rothstein, the managing partner and CEO of the firm, has, according to assertions of certain investors, allegedly orchestrated a substantial misappropriation of funds from investor trust accounts that made use of the law firm's name. The investment business created and operated by Rothstein centered on the sale of interests in structured settlements. Immediate judicial action is being sought to facilitate the investigation and accounting of investor funds and to address the ongoing affairs of the firm in an appropriate manner.

The motion continued:

Firm lawyers learned in the past few days about irregularities surrounding a settlement funding business operated by Rothstein.

The settlement funding business involved the purchase of structured legal settlements and the sale of these settlements to investors. Various investors have informed the firm that they believe that substantial funds are not properly accounted for and are missing. A review of the firm's records undertaken over this past weekend indicates that various funds unrelated to the direct practice of law cannot be accounted for, circumstances suggesting that investor money may have been misused by Rothstein who controlled all such accounts. Some investors allege that Defendant Rothstein may have been fabricating non-existent structured legal settlements for sale to investors.

With all the chaos from the fallout of the imploding firm came a message from Scott Rothstein's attorney stating Rothstein intended to return to South Florida to "straighten things out." They seemed like the shallow words of a pathetic liar.

Though all were working hard to distance themselves from Rothstein, he used his connections right up to the end. He left not just on any plane; he boarded a chartered G-5 jet, rented from Governor Charlie Crist's wife's ex-husband's company, according to Bob Norman's November 5, 2009, article on his blog *The Daily Pulp*.

It also seemed that Rothstein did not take the usual path that the ordinary traveler would take from his car to the plane. According to Amy Sherman and Jay Weaver's article in the November 7, 2009, *Miami Herald*, Scott Rothstein "[contacted] Broward sheriff's executive officer, Lt. David Benjamin, to escort him from his car to the airplane at Fort Lauderdale Executive Airport." The article indicated that the sheriff's spokesman, Jim Leljedal, confirmed that indeed that was the case.

According to *SunSentinel.com*'s writer, Brittany Wallman, in an article posted on November 12, 2009, Sheriff Al Lamberti removed Benjamin from his role overseeing internal affairs shortly after it was learned he assisted Rothstein's flight from the country. Lt. Benjamin worked for the Broward Sheriff's Office and was a "close friend" of

Rothstein according to Bob Norman's November 24, 2009, column on his blog; titled "Source: BSO Lieutenant's Office Received $30,000 from Rothstein."

The article indicated that the lieutenant "received $30,000 from Scott Rothstein for his outside consulting firm, DWB Consulting Group, a Delaware Company Incorporated in Florida in May with the help of then-RRA attorney Christina Kitterman."

Clearly, it was a good idea that I hadn't called the Broward Sheriff's Office requesting an investigation of Scott Rothstein. Rothstein did not have a monopoly on getting help to an awaiting airplane, though in the case of my neighbor, in the following story, "Get to the Head of the Line," the help he received wasn't due to patronage, but kindness.

Get to the Head of the Line

Jonathan Stern had worked for weeks to set up important appointments with a number of prominent rabbis and leaders in Israel to help jumpstart a new charitable project he was developing. Jonathan was excited since the trip was just twenty-four hours away. He was also taking items to Israel for many of his friends and neighbors who had sons and daughters learning in Israel.

His suits were pressed, gifts were wrapped, and final preparations were made to be sure he had everything necessary. As he opened his passport with just twenty hours until takeoff, he grew faint as he realized his passport had expired less than a week before. *What in the world can be done?* he thought to himself. How was he to get from Miami to Jerusalem? He called everywhere and still had no idea how he could get a new passport in time for the flight. Quickly, ideas went through his mind. He knew that with a little effort he could reschedule all of the appointments. But he also realized that his ticket was non-refundable and he could not afford to buy another one. Eager to learn what could be done, he prayed with a little extra concentration. He grabbed a large cup of steaming hot coffee, checking only to be sure that it was not decaffeinated, then off he went to the passport office and waited an hour for the office to open.

Jonathan explained his situation to the clerk and asked that they expedite his re-issuance of his passport in time for his flight. The clerk explained that Jonathan needed to go to El Al Israel Airlines, get a form signed and bring it back immediately. That one signed form was all that Jonathan needed and he would be on his way to the airport with his passport in hand. *Simple enough*, Jonathan thought. El Al obliged and quickly signed the form. Jonathan raced back to the passport office, believing he would actually make his flight. After parking his car as close as possible, which was not close at all, he ran to the office and opened the door. The place was packed. It appeared everyone had decided to renew their passport at the same time.

Jonathan explained his situation to the guard – that the passport office sent him to get a paper signed and come right back. But the guard insisted that he take a number and wait his turn like everyone else. Jonathan saw someone else grab the next number. The last person being served was number 76 and Jonathan's number was 178; there were more than 100 people ahead of him! His pacing up and back and the expression of bewilderment on his face made it clear to Shmuel Selmar, who recognized him from his neighborhood, that something was wrong. He did not know Jonathan but he knew he lived in the community. Shmuel was not sure what, if anything, he could do to help but he was not about to give up the opportunity to try.

Shmuel walked over to Mr. Stern, approximately twenty years his senior, and greeted him with a smile and a pleasant word and asked if something were wrong – knowing already something was, he was just not sure what. Mr. Stern explained his situation. Shmuel immediately responded that his number was 79 and suggested they trade numbers and everything would be perfect. Taken aback by Shmuel's genuine and spontaneous act of kindness, Jonathan said, "That helps me but you will be here for at least another hour. That is not right."

Shmuel said, "I do not mind waiting another hour, if it will help get you on your plane."

Jonathan felt uncomfortable trading numbers and setting Shmuel Selmar back an hour or more, but he knew it was his only hope of making his flight. Twenty minutes later, Jonathan was running out the door with his passport in hand. Jonathan got back to the airport just in time for his flight and he was on his way to Israel. The excitement of the trip was magnified by the kindness Shmuel had extended to him.

So much good can be done, if one is kind enough to give an hour of one's time. Even without the type of "official" escort Scott Rothstein had, Jonathan felt like a valued human being because of Shmuel's sensitivity to his plight.

Chapter 14

A Sinking Ship

*The everyday kindness of the
back roads more than makes up for
the acts of greed in the headlines.*

~CHARLES KURALT

O N *SUNSENTINEL.COM* on November 2, 2009, staff writers Jon Burstein, Sally Kestin, and Scott Wyman wrote, of Rothstein: "He's been away to clear his head."

Rothstein's criminal defense attorney, Marc Nurik, stated, "Scott's out of town for a short period of time. He was always going to be returning at the end of the week. He didn't flee anywhere. His intention is to straighten this thing out."

Few people believed that Rothstein would return to the United States, and hardly anyone believed he could straighten out the mess. It took him four-and-a-half years and 1.4 billion dollars to get *into* such a huge amount of trouble. It would not be easy to straighten it out even in a hundred years. Furthermore, Rothstein was in a country that did not have an extradition treaty with the United States and he had $16,000,000 cash and millions of dollars of watches with him. Why would Rothstein come back? He would probably face the rest of his life, or nearly the rest of his life, in jail even if he cooperated.

But the flamboyant, unpredictable, self-destructive con man

extraordinaire did return on Tuesday, November 3, 2009. Scottie was filmed saying, "I'm going to make it right …. People make mistakes in life. You make a mistake, you fix it." But if he really regretted what he did and not just getting caught, why did Rothstein return to the United States in a chartered private jet paid for with stolen money rather than in a significantly less expensive coach seat on a scheduled airliner?

Everyone speculated what the real reason was for his return. The most logical explanation seemed to be one of the following choices: Scott Rothstein was delusional and believed that if he came back and apologized and started turning in a lot of other people who were part of his scam or engaged in other illegal conduct, he would get a very short sentence. Alternatively, Rothstein may have believed he would be far safer in jail than on the run. With investors losing hundreds of millions of dollars he may have concluded or even been told that they would find him and take him apart, piece by piece. At that point, jail might have started sounding pretty good.

Word was that Scott Rothstein was meeting with the U.S. Attorney's Office and the FBI. The general public presumed that in the hopes of a lighter sentence and better accommodations, Scott was naming names of people who had helped him commit the massive fraud. According to Rothstein's attorney, Marc Nurik, Rothstein was assisting the government in locating all of his property, but that was the extent of his involvement. To many it seemed odd that Rothstein was videotaped having a martini at one of his usual spots, The Capital Grille, rather than in prison on November 9, 2009. He repeated several times, "I'm going to do the right thing."

For the next three weeks he remained free but no doubt under the careful watch of the FBI. There were rumors that Rothstein was trying to bring someone down in order to get a lighter sentence, but again, they were just rumors.

On another front, Rothstein had begun trying to mend fences with his people. In a November 4, 2009, article on *SunSentinel.com*,

Jon Burstein, Paula McMahon, and Brittany Wallman reported that while Rothstein was out of the country, he had texted the following to four of his partners:

"Sorry for letting you all down. I'm a fool. I thought I could fix it but got trapped by my ego and refusal to fail and now all I have accomplished is hurting the people I love. Please take care of yourselves and please protect Kimmie [Rothstein's wife]. She knew nothing. Neither did she nor any of you deserve what I did. I hope G-d allows me to see you on the other side.

Love, Scott."

According to the article, Rothstein had told Rosenfeldt on October 31 that he felt he had three options: "kill himself, live life on the lam as a fugitive, or go to prison and risk being killed there because he has made enemies." The article went on to say that Rosenfeldt urged him, "Choose life."

Turning back to the practice of law, the RRA law firm ended that day with a new leader at its helm. On November 3, 2009, the Court granted the firm's petition to appoint a receiver,[6] and Judge Streitfeld appointed retired Miami-Dade Circuit Court Judge Herbert Stettin. Judge Stettin was assigned the responsibility for the firm's day-to-day financial decisions. Co-founding partner Stuart Rosenfeldt remained responsible for the legal decisions. Scott Rothstein was removed as the Chairman, CEO and managing partner.

Rosenfeldt became the CEO and managing partner of a quickly sinking ship without a compass. On November 3, 2009, *worldlawdirect.com* reported this about Stuart Rosenfeldt: "Mr. Rosenfeldt says he will seek to reconstitute the law firm without Mr. Rothstein. The firm now faces cash shortages. Mr. Rosenfeldt says he 'deposited two-thirds of my life savings in my firm's operating account' to prop up finances in the short term."

---

6 A receiver is a person appointed by a court to manage the affairs of a bankrupt or insolvent business and to locate and care for whatever property the business has.

A couple of weeks later, Rosenfeldt named Judge Stettin the CRO, chief restructuring officer, making Judge Stettin responsible for operating the firm but retaining the right to terminate him. Several days after that Stuart Rosenfeldt resigned from the firm and moved out of his office.

Just before leaving the country, Rothstein was said to have wired $16,000,000 to himself and two other individuals in Casablanca. A week after RRA had a receiver appointed in Florida State Court, it found itself heading toward the U.S. Bankruptcy Court in Fort Lauderdale. Attorneys John Genovese and Jeffrey Sonn, representing three creditors whose claims totaled just under $700,000, filed the involuntary bankruptcy. Genovese and Sonn were concerned about 1.4 million dollars deposited in a trust account which, after Rothstein left town, was transferred into the firm's operating account. Judge Stettin was then named trustee in the bankruptcy case.

Among the first actions Judge Stettin took as bankruptcy trustee was to request that thirty charities, which had received money from Rothstein's firm, return the money within ten days or face legal action. As the letter was going out, charities all around town were taking down Rothstein's name from buildings and portions of buildings named after him. It might have been more appropriate to circle his name and put a line through it, thus letting Rothstein be remembered for what he was, a villain who destroyed himself and gave decent people the opportunity to destroy themselves. His actions showed that he did not care about hurting even the people that he knew, including his partners and his wife.

In my community, there are people whose actions show that they care about people that they do not even know.

Around the Clock!

It was Wednesday, February 14, 2007, late in the evening, when Yitzi Rosenberg and Yona Lunger each received a call from a different person telling of *Sam Cohen*, an eighty-year old gentleman, a Holocaust survivor with memory problems who had wandered off and could not be located. Mr. Cohen's wife did not know who to turn to. She and her husband were in Miami Beach on vacation. The Miami Beach Police were called and offered invaluable assistance, as did many members of the Miami Beach community. That night and the next night, Yitzi, Yona, and dozens of volunteers worked through the nights.

On a regular basis, Yitzi Rosenberg, the head of *Shmira* (the volunteer neighborhood patrol) in North Miami Beach, along with his friend Yona Lunger, are among the first to be called when there is a suspicious incident or after a crime occurs. Whenever they are around, they respond and do whatever they can. Often they also patrol the neighborhood at night. When needed outside the community, they are just as fast to respond.

Dovid Cohen shared with me the thoughts running through his mind as Yitzi and Yona led a group of at times up to eighty volunteers looking to find his missing father, *Sam Cohen*. Dovid told me Yitzi did not make much conversation with him as they drove searching for Dovid's father.

"But," Dovid said, "Yitzi was making call after call, organizing volunteers, and discussing what else needed to be done. He did not say much to me, but he did a lot." Dovid said that when he was driving with Yitzi he "gained confidence that everything possible that could be done was being done."

He said, "The fact that Yitzi and so many other volunteers would put in so many hours looking for a person from outside of Florida that they did not know is beyond belief. They did not even know the family. Yitzi was adamant that thousands of flyers needed to be given out and that someone would recognize my father from them and call the police, and that is exactly what happened."

"When I drove with Yona, Yona was just so upbeat, I knew my father would be found. I can tell you it was so important to hear from someone with such a positive attitude that my father would be found and he would be fine. That, combined with seeing how much

Yitzi was doing, was an enormous relief," explained Dovid Cohen. "While Yitzi and Yona had different approaches to comforting me, the combination of both was very effective."

Yitzi immediately created a missing-person flyer with the photo of Sam Cohen, and arranged for a command center to be established at the last known location of Mr. Cohen: the intersection of 69th Street and Collins Avenue in Miami Beach, near Publix supermarket.

As the search began, three Miami Beach Police detectives arrived at the command center. They assisted with advice, strategies, and the search itself. Volunteers and police canvassed neighborhood stores, hospitals, bus stops, gathering places for homeless people, and hotels within an eight block radius of the command center.

The search continued non-stop for over thirty-six hours with few leads. Family had begun to arrive from as far away as Israel. Private detectives were hired but there were still no leads. As word got out, more and more offers of help came in. An out-of-town trainer of search dogs arranged to send two K-9 search dogs to join the effort. Arrangements were made for dozens of ATVs to be used by the members of the search party, allowing them to search the beach and other remote locations as well as provide additional visibility for the search efforts.

On Friday morning, February 16, the words everyone was praying they would soon hear, were heard: "Mr. Sam Cohen was located."

A security guard saw him in a room at a hotel that was being renovated and recognized him from a flyer as the missing person. Sam Cohen was in good health and was reunited with his family, thanks to Yitzi Rosenberg, Yona Lunger, the Miami Beach Police, the guard who located Mr. Cohen, and dozens of volunteers from the Miami Beach and the North Miami Beach communities.

Dovid Cohen had nothing but praise for the people of North Miami Beach and Miami Beach. The concerns shown by volunteers for a stranger reflects the deep commitment to helping each other that exists in my community.

Chapter 15

Winning with Integrity is Everything

*You can have everything in life
you want, if you will just help
other people get what they want.*

~ZIG ZIGLAR

ONE THING FOR SURE regarding Scott Rothstein is that he was an equal opportunity scam artist. He had no loyalty, no concern and, now, no friends. There is an old joke – how can you tell if an attorney is lying? The answer is, when his lips are moving. As a general rule, I certainly hope this is not true. Unfortunately, this scam artist fit the bill well. Whenever Rothstein spoke, there was a steady stream of lies. His conduct was the lowest of the low, yet it got even lower. In the days after he fled, such conduct became clearer, and more publicized, by the day.

According to a story that appeared in the *Miami Herald* on December 11, 2009, Ed Morse, an eighty-eight-year-old owner of fifteen auto dealerships, and his wife Carol, had hired their "good friend" Scott Rothstein to handle a legal matter. A Broward County interior designer had charged the Morses nearly $2,000,000 for design work in two of their homes. The Morses were not satisfied with the quality of the work and some of the "add on" charges and, therefore, filed suit through the master scammer, Scott Rothstein. The case did not go exactly as Scott Rothstein had hoped. In fact, the Morses lost and the interior decorator filed a counterclaim to the lawsuit and was awarded $800,000. It happens. Cases are lost for various reasons. Sometimes the case is weak. Other times there is conflicting evidence and the court is not convinced. Still other times an attorney does a poor job representing the client.

For Scottie Rothstein, however, losing was not an option. By now Scottie had perfected the art of deception and had become quite skilled at falsifying any document. The federal judge in the case said that the Morses lost. But a few minutes on Scottie's computer solved that problem! Rothstein's masterpiece and the Morses' nightmare now showed a completely fabricated judgment in favor of Ed and Carol Morse in the amount of $23,000.000.

Scott Rothstein wasn't content with just winning; he needed to win big. For whatever reason, he was afraid to tell the Morses that he had lost or he felt there was a tremendous opportunity to bring in more money by telling them he won. Unconcerned that the Morses might wonder how they won $23,000,000 when they only paid under $2,000,000 for the work, Rothstein sent the Morses the new, improved, phony, final judgment for $23,000,000.

Taking a break from his Ponzi scheme for a moment with the Morses, Scottie tried his hand at the "Nigerian email" scam. You know the one to which I am referring. You probably receive one a week or, if you are fortunate, only one a month. This is the annoying Nigerian email notifying the recipient that he won money, received an inheritance, or was being asked to help assist the sender of the email in funneling money from Nigeria to another country. It must be that the Nigerian payment scam actually works, or by now the scammers would have moved on to something else.

According to the *Miami Herald*, Rothstein told the Morses that the interior designer had a bank account in the Cayman Islands. As in the Nigeria scenarios, there was a hitch. To get the money out of the Cayman Islands, Scottie told the Morses they needed to post a $57,000,000 bond.

Therefore, Scott Rothstein requested that the Morses wire to RRA's trust account $57 million. The Morses went for the scheme, hook, line, and sinker. They obviously trusted Scott Rothstein since he was their attorney and a "close friend," or so they thought. The situation makes me wonder if the day has come when you need to hire an attorney to represent you in speaking to your primary attorney. Scott has degraded the legal profession and will forever make it tougher for clients to believe in lawyers. It's a shame that a small but growing number of scoundrels could stain the reputation of such a noble profession but, because that is the case, it is even more incumbent upon people to report unscrupulous behavior as soon as it is witnessed.

Scott Rothstein, the master juggler, had to do everything possible to keep his clients from ever coming into contact with the interior designer, the attorney for the interior designer, the court mediator or the judge. He was forever juggling whatever was necessary to keep this from happening. He obtained continuance[7] after continuance with ridiculous excuse after ridiculous excuse. Time ran out, though, on October 27, 2009. That was the day the interior designer's attorney had scheduled a hearing to hold the Morses in contempt of court for failure to sign the settlement documents that were agreed to, presumably by Scottie Rothstein on behalf of his clients. Of course, on October 27, Rothstein was en route to Morocco to "clear his head."

Not only did Scott Rothstein not treat his "close friends" Ed and Carol Morse properly, he didn't even treat them as well as those he ripped off in the Ponzi scheme. In the Ponzi scheme, Scottie was paying "investors" more than 100 percent on their money each year, some over 200 percent, and a select few over 300 percent. So why didn't Scottie at least return the $57,000,000 to the Morses a year later plus pay the $23,000,000 "judgment," and for good measure

---

7 An extension of time granted by a court.

pay $800,000 to the interior designer? If he did that after a year, he would have been paying them less than forty-two percent per annum on their money. That's an absolute bargain in Rothstein's ludicrous world of thievery and, of course, it could all be accomplished by stealing from the next "investor/victim." Scottie did not extend that courtesy to the Morses probably because they were "good friends." They trusted him and they were not chasing after him with a chainsaw, like, no doubt, his investors would be if he missed a payment by several months or a year.

On December 12, 2009, Edward and Carol Morse filed suit against Rothstein and other partners of the RRA firm for professional malpractice and breach of fiduciary duty[8], among other things. Their lawsuit relates to the above-mentioned case against the interior designer as well as to other cases handled or should I say "mishandled" by Rothstein on the Morses' behalf.

Did Rothstein really enjoy his victories? It is doubtful. They were all meaningless. When a person is chasing honor and attention, he can never get enough. He concentrates on what is missing, not on what he gets. He also knows deep down he does not own his victories.

"Did Bassie Save *Shabbos* or Did *Shabbos* Save Bassie?" is another great story from our community, and an excellent example of living with one's heart on the right side and understanding that winning at any cost is not winning.

Did Bassie Save *Shabbos* or Did *Shabbos* Save Bassie?

On Saturday night, February 23, 2008, at 6:15 P.M., the Florida High School Athletic Association Queen of the Hill three-point shooting competition was about to start. Only one of the state's top two high school basketball stars in the girls' division was present. No one was surprised. Everyone knew Bassie Orzechowitz, a senior

---

8 A fiduciary duty is an obligation to act in the best interest of another party, such as an attorney for his client. When one person does agree to act for another in a fiduciary relationship, the law forbids the fiduciary from acting in any manner adverse or contrary to the interests of the other party, or from acting for his own benefit in relation to the subject matter. If he does, he has breached his fiduciary duty.

at Weinbaum Yeshiva High School, in Boca Raton, Florida, was a *Shabbos* observant Jew.

Bassie worked long and hard to be Florida's best female three-point shooter. Winning would also have meant advancing to the nationals, a dream for any seventeen-year-old. So where was Bassie? Why wasn't she willing to give up just one *Shabbos* or even just a few minutes of one *Shabbos* for a real shot at winning the state title and a chance at the national championship?

To Bassie, basketball was a passion, an important passion, but Judaism is a way of life and *Shabbos* is the crown of Judaism. Trading *Shabbos* for the state championship was never a consideration for Bassie. She would have loved to have had both but if she could only pick one, without any hesitation, *Shabbos* was her choice.

In my book Bassie was a big winner in many ways. In a world where so many young people only think about themselves, she put G-d first and sanctified His name before the tens of thousands of people who read her story in one of many newspapers or on the web or saw it on television. She served as a great role model for youngsters by showing them that "how you win" is more important than winning itself. The lesson is clear; you do not sacrifice your core beliefs to advance your personal goals. It's a great lesson and it was well taught. How easy it is to say what we would do if we were faced with the challenge, but Bassie was put to the test and passed!

Those fifteen three-pointer shots Bassie did not take, since the Florida High School Athletic Association would not wait the few minutes for *Shabbos* to end, will not be forgotten. At that moment, Bassie made G-d important and relevant for everyone to see. Since G-d deals with us measure for measure, it is my guess that when sometime, or maybe fifteen sometimes in the future something seems a little out of reach to Bassie, The Creator of All will remember the day when the three-pointers were within her reach and so was the state championship but Bassie made His will hers. It will be then that He makes her will His.

As outstanding as Bassie's conduct was in this incident, she has a character trait even more impressive. Bassie lives a block away from us and has been close friends with one of our daughters for years, so she has been to our house quite a bit, especially during the years they attended the same school. I remember commenting to my wife that I never heard Bassie even once utter an unkind word, even in jest, about anyone. Now, that is unusual in this day and age.

Sanctifying G-d's name and not looking for faults in others is the combination that will bring G-d's presence closer to us all. Bassie represented *Torah* well and her community is very proud of her.

As beautiful as what Bassie did for *Shabbos*, now let me tell you what *Shabbos* did for Bassie. The evening after she forfeited the event, Bassie was rushed to the hospital and had emergency surgery to have her appendix removed. Thank G-d, she recovered nicely. Doctors pointed out that a short delay or more exertion could have caused Bassie's appendix to rupture.

Imagine if Bassie's opponent were to have said, "Let's wait the fifteen minutes for Bassie's Sabbath to be over. I want to win, but I also respect her right to observe her Sabbath." Bassie's opponent still may have won, but envision what a victory it would have been for her to win with such class. Picture how G-d would have felt if He were put first by both sides.

In my community people have their priorities straight and will not consider sacrificing friendships, beliefs, or values for personal gain. Scott Rothstein would never understand the strength of such people shown by standing steadfast to their value systems.

Chapter 16

The Cast of Characters

"Oh! what a tangled web we weave, when
first we practise to deceive!"

~Sir Walter Scott, "Marmion"

O N NOVEMBER 17, 2008, on *SunSentinel.com*, colum-
nist Michael Mayo had quoted attorney William R.
Sherer, a luminary in South Florida Republican Party
politics, about Rothstein: "Whatever he's doing, it's
working ... I chose his firm [RRA] as my lawyers, to represent me in
some attorney-fee litigation cases. That should tell you something."

One year and four days later the tables turned. On November
20, 2009, attorney William R. Scherer, a principal of the law firm
Conrad and Scherer, LLP, filed a 147-page lawsuit against Rothstein
and others believed to be involved in Rothstein's 1.4-billion-dollar
Ponzi scheme. Less than a week later, with more information avail-
able, a 289-page, 238-count amended complaint was filed which
included more parties. On April 20, 2010, a 1,329-page, 1263-
count second amended complaint was filed including still more
parties. The suit opens an additional window into the operations of
the colossal scandal and what took place during the final hours. The
plaintiffs[9] invested over $120,000,000 in Rothstein's Ponzi scheme.

---

9 The parties bringing suit to recover their money.

From those documents and others filed in the case, a cast of characters emerges befitting of inclusion in a John Grisham novel. The cast included the following key defendants[10] and many others not listed below. All quotations are from the amended complaint and/or second amended complaint:

> **Barry R. Bekkedam** ... the chief executive officer and president of [a fund that invested in Rothstein's scheme]. Bekkedam materially participated, conspired, assisted, encouraged, and otherwise aided and abetted one or more of the other defendants in the unlawful, misleading, and fraudulent conduct alleged herein while willfully ignoring and/or failing to exercise reasonable care.
>
> **Gary Berkowitz** ... a certified public accountant of Berenfeld Spritzer Shechter Sheer, LLP (Berenfeld). Berkowitz materially participated, conspired, assisted, encouraged, and otherwise aided and abetted one or more of the other defendants in the unlawful, misleading, and fraudulent conduct alleged herein while willfully ignoring and/or failing to exercise reasonable care.
>
> **David Boden** ... a shareholder and general counsel for RRA. Boden was Rothstein's "right-hand man" and an essential participant in the scheme by, among other things, participating in investor inducement meetings, negotiating and drafting the putative settlement and assignment documents, acting as the "closing agent" to secure investor funding, and advising and soliciting investors into funding settlements despite actual and/or constructive knowledge that the investments were part of a Ponzi scheme. Boden materially participated, conspired, assisted, encouraged, and otherwise aided and abetted one or more of the other defendants in the unlawful, misleading, and fraudulent conduct alleged herein while willfully ignoring and/or failing to exercise reasonable care.
>
> **George G. Levin** ... the chief executive officer and managing member of ... [various funds]. Levin, who previously owned and

---

10 Those being sued.

operated GGL Industries, Inc. d/b/a Classic Motor Carriages, a company convicted of federal fraud charges, actively participated in the scheme by, among other things, recruiting, inducing, conspiring, assisting, encouraging, and otherwise aiding and abetting one or more of the other defendants in the unlawful, misleading, and fraudulent conduct alleged herein while willfully ignoring and/or failing to exercise reasonable care. Similar to his operation of Classic Motor Carriages, Levin relied on others in [an investment fund] to do his "dirty work" in an attempt to insulate him[self] from both criminal and civil liability. Levin's participation in the Ponzi scheme should be considered "Classic Motors 2.0."

Richard Pearson ... the sole owner and president of R.L. Pearson. Pearson participated in the scheme by actively serving as a "feeder" that materially participated, conspired, assisted, encouraged, and otherwise aided and abetted one or more of the other defendants in the unlawful, misleading, and fraudulent conduct alleged herein while willfully ignoring and/or failing to exercise reasonable care.

Frank J. Preve ... the chief operating officer or agent of ... [various funds]. Preve maintained an office at RRA and was the key ... [fund] insider who devoted significant time and effort collaborating with Rothstein to operate the Ponzi. Preve, a convicted bank fraud and embezzlement felon, ... participated in the scheme by, among other things, recruiting, inducing, conspiring, assisting, encouraging, and otherwise aiding and abetting one or more of the other defendants in the unlawful, misleading, and fraudulent conduct alleged herein while willfully ignoring and/or failing to exercise reasonable care. Preve also acted as the first level of insulation between his boss, Levin, and the fraud being committed by Rothstein. A footnote in the lawsuit states, Frank Preve pled guilty to bank embezzlement charges in 1985 and received ten years probation and a $10,000 fine for falsifying loan documents in connection with a scheme that resulted in losses exceeding $2,300,000.

Frank Spinosa ... a senior vice-president of operations for TD Bank. Spinosa contributed to the scheme by, among other things, meeting with investors, providing falsified account statements, preparing irrevocable "lock letters," and using his position at the bank to induce investor funding. Additionally, Spinosa materially participated, conspired, assisted, encouraged, and otherwise aided and abetted one or more of the other defendants in the unlawful, misleading, and fraudulent conduct alleged herein while willfully ignoring and/or failing to exercise reasonable care. On or about November, 2009, TD Bank terminated Spinosa's employment.

Irene Stay ... the chief financial officer of RRA. Stay participated in the scheme by furnishing investors with falsified bank account statements and wire transfer confirmations used to induce investor funding despite having actual or constructive knowledge that the investments were a Ponzi scheme. Stay materially participated, conspired, assisted, encouraged, and otherwise aided and abetted one or more of the other defendants in the unlawful, misleading, and fraudulent conduct alleged herein while willfully ignoring and/or failing to exercise reasonable care.

Michael Szafranski ... the president of Onyx Options Consultants Corporation (Onyx) and ABS Capital Funding, LLC (ABS). Szafranski was hired as an "independent" third party on behalf of [funds] and was tasked with verifying the legitimacy of the purported confidential settlements. Specifically, Szafranski was the only person vested with authority to analyze the unredacted settlement documents, to substantiate the putative plaintiffs' and putative defendants' existence, to confirm the putative defendants' pre-funded wire transfer into the Principal Conspirators' TD Bank escrow account, to verify the Principal Conspirators' TD Bank trust and escrow account balances, and to provide an opinion as to the authenticity of the settlement deals. Szafranski participated in the scheme by, among other things, making material misrepresentations, false verifications, and conspiring to induce investor funding while accepting over $32,000,000 in payments from the Principal

Conspirators despite having actual or constructive knowledge that the investments were a Ponzi scheme. Szafranski materially participated, conspired, assisted, encouraged, and otherwise aided and abetted one or more of the other defendants in the unlawful, misleading, and fraudulent conduct alleged herein while willfully ignoring and/or failing to exercise reasonable care. [Szafranski received $6,480,000.00] ... in Ponzi money from the Principal Conspirators between July 9, 2009, and October 23, 2009.

It is perfectly possible to function as a third-party verifier, although an earlier chapter of this book notes that the independent verification process assumed the authenticity of all documents and data provided by Rothstein to Szafranski. The reason seemed to be that the verifier or his clients believed Rothstein's integrity was beyond reproach based upon all of the leaders vouching for him and his being appointed to key positions.

It is also perfectly possible to bring in investors and to be paid for doing so. But it is not possible to do both at the same time. Once you invest, or bring in any investor, you are no longer independent. You lose your objectivity. As the saying goes, "You can't dance at two weddings at the same time."

Furthermore, a pleading filed in the case by the plaintiffs paints a picture of a very close, cozy relationship between Rothstein and Szafranski. The pleading shows that Szafranski, the "independent third-party verifier," was beginning to write emails like Rothstein did with the "Love yas" and the last letter of the first name repeated numerous times. It seemed that Rothstein was Szafranski's mentor who he trusted implicitly.

Debra E. Villegas ... the chief operating officer at RRA. Villegas, Rothstein's proclaimed number two at RRA, participated in the scheme by, among other things, drafting and notarizing fallacious putative settlement and assignment agreements, furnishing investors with false bank account statements and fictitious wire transfer notifications for the purpose of inducing investments into the

Ponzi scheme despite having actual or constructive knowledge of same. Villegas materially participated, conspired, assisted, encouraged, and otherwise aided and abetted one or more of the other defendants in the unlawful, misleading, and fraudulent conduct alleged herein while willfully ignoring and/or failing to exercise reasonable care.

Tracy Weintraub ... the senior audit and managing partner of Berenfeld's Fort Lauderdale office located in the same building as RRA. Weintraub materially participated, conspired, assisted, encouraged, and otherwise aided and abetted one or more of the other defendants in the unlawful, misleading, and fraudulent conduct alleged herein while willfully ignoring and/or failing to exercise reasonable care.

BERENFELD SPRITZER SHECHTER SHEER, LLP ... served as the auditing firm for [various funds] and as the accounting firm for RRA and Rothstein individually. As described, Berenfeld was uniquely positioned as auditor [for funds that invested with Rothstein] and RRA's accountant to discover the fraudulent scheme and, despite countless "red flags" failed to do so. Berenfeld's unqualified audit opinion of [funds], which it knew was being incorporated into a Confidential Offering Memorandum, authenticating hundreds of millions of dollars of non-existent receivables, was so patently deficient that the audit amounted to no audit at all. Berenfeld materially participated, conspired, assisted, encouraged, and otherwise aided and abetted one or more of the other defendants in the unlawful, misleading, and fraudulent conduct alleged herein while willfully ignoring and/or failing to exercise reasonable care.

GIBRALTAR PRIVATE BANK & TRUST, CO. ... a private bank and wealth management firm ... Gibraltar Bank violated internal procedures and policies in providing the Principal Conspirators with special overdraft accommodations, blindly authorizing numerous suspicious money transfers and disregarding apparent fraud warning signs. Gibraltar Bank materially participated, conspired, assisted, encouraged, and otherwise aided and abetted one or more of the other defendants in the unlawful, misleading, and fraudulent conduct alleged herein while willfully ignoring and/or failing to exercise reasonable care.

R.L. PEARSON AND ASSOCIATES, INC. ... owned and operated by its president and sole officer, Richard Pearson. R.L. Pearson participated in the scheme by actively serving as a "feeder" entity which materially participated, conspired, assisted, encouraged, and otherwise aided and abetted one or more of the other defendants in the unlawful, misleading, and fraudulent conduct alleged herein while willfully ignoring and/or failing to exercise reasonable care.

TD BANK ... a foreign national banking association. ... TD Bank was the financial epicenter of the Ponzi scheme as hundreds of millions, if not billions, of Ponzi dollars flowed through RRA's TD Bank escrow, trust, and operating accounts. Despite the grossly inordinate amount of funds being rapidly wired in and out of RRA's accounts held at two local South Florida branches, these suspicious account activities inexplicably circumvented several fraud-risk tripwires and avoided detection by TD Bank's internal bank compliance officers and systems. TD Bank knowingly, recklessly, or with willful blindness conspired and/or aided and abetted the fraudulent misappropriation of investor funds or otherwise negligently disregarded countless warning signs evidencing the scam. As asserted herein, TD Bank lent credibility to the legitimacy of the Ponzi scheme and materially participated, conspired, assisted, encouraged, and otherwise aided and abetted one or more of the other defendants in the unlawful, misleading, and fraudulent conduct alleged. TD Bank also deliberately ignored and/or failed to exercise the reasonable care required of a similarly situated bank.

The lawsuit refers to Scott Rothstein and RRA as the Principal Conspirators. The lawsuit also calls (TD Bank, Spinosa, Gibraltar Bank, Berenfeld, Weintraub, Berkowitz, Levin, Preve, [investment funds], Villegas, Boden, Stay, and others) "the Principal Conspirators' inner-circle of facilitators" and (TD Bank, Spinosa, Levin, Preve, Szafranski, Onyx, ABS, Bekkedam, Pearson, R.L. Pearson [investment funds], and others) as "promoters" that "were essential to the perpetration of this systemic fraud ...."

Further demonstrating that Rothstein did not act alone, the lawsuit points to Rothstein's interview with the *Sun-Sentinel* on November 23, 2009, in which Rothstein is quoted as saying that karma had caught up with him, "but it will catch up with others, too .... You're in a town full of thieves and, at the end of the day, everyone will see. I'll leave it at that."

The suit asserts that the defendants engaged in the stated conduct despite having actual knowledge that the investments were a Ponzi scheme.

Noticeably absent from the list of defendants is the RRA law firm, even though the firm is referred to as one of the Principal Conspirators. By the date of filing of the lawsuit, the firm was rapidly vanishing. While it was still in operation, reports later indicated the firm was operating at a huge deficit. Ponzi money was said to be making up the shortfall. RRA's actual value at the time of the lawsuit could have only been a larger negative number. Also, considering that RRA had filed bankruptcy, naming the firm would also have required relief from the automatic stay by the Bankruptcy Court.[11] The suit did refer to the firm as a "front" for the Ponzi scheme. The firm was purported to be handling the legal disputes that were settled and available for sale. The Plaintiffs' Second Amended Complaint continues:

> By October 30, 2009, investors began to scramble desperately attempting to reach Rothstein for answers. Unbeknownst to them, Rothstein was already gone [to Morocco], along with their investments, as the Ponzi scheme finally buckled under the pressure of obligations due.

---

11 When a party files bankruptcy, certain things are automatically "stayed," or prohibited, during the bankruptcy case. Among other things, the automatic stay prohibits beginning or continuing a lawsuit against the debtor, unless the bankruptcy judge lifts the stay.

Alarmed investors frantically reached out to RRA executives and attorneys begging for information as to the whereabouts of Rothstein and their more than $30,000,000 in overdue payments. Stuart Rosenfeldt assembled a team including Boden, Stay, and Grant Smith [Smith was an RRA partner promoted in October 2009 to assistant managing shareholder, and he apparently had signatory authority on some RRA accounts], at RRA to begin answering the deluge of investor calls by first confirming with Stay (RRA's CFO) that RRA's operating and trust accounts contained more than one billion dollars.

Shamefully, Stay refused to provide Rosenfeldt the confirmation requested. Growing ever agitated, Rosenfeldt and the others continued to press Stay, demanding to know what was going on and that she produce current account statements. Eventually Stay relented and began inconsolably crying, repeating the phrase, "I don't want to go to jail." Rosenfeldt proceeded to conference call Frank Spinosa, senior vice-president at TD Bank, who initially declined to provide account balance verification but after much cajoling finally informed Rosenfeldt that the RRA accounts had been almost completely depleted.

[O]n November 1, 2009, Mel Lifshitz of DE Securities, whose group invested nearly $100,000,000. into the Ponzi scheme, advised a group of investor victims that he personally sat with Spinosa at TD Bank and verified investment account balances .... The group of investors attending the November 1, 2009, meeting include[d]: Dean Kretschmar, Ted Morse, Ed Morse, Richard Pearson, Ira Sochet, Mel Lifshitz, A.J. Discala, Mac Melvin, Mark Nordlicht, Jack Simony, Steve Jackel, Laurence King, Steve Levin, George Levin, Frank Preve, Barry Bekkedam, and Michael Szafranski.

[D]uring that same meeting, Levin informed the group that he reached out to Rothstein in Morocco letting him know that [a fund of his] stood ready to provide shortfall financing if he was having trouble making payments. Astoundingly, Levin's revealing admission took the group by surprise because one of the core "deal" tenets insured against any possible deficit by requiring a putative defendant's settlement to be funded prior to an investor's lump sum purchase. Thus, any shortfall, even the smallest one, is patently contrary to the investment structure and obvious evidence that the monies are either being misused or are a part of a Ponzi scheme.

Plaintiffs who filed suit in this matter "now believed that Levin's statement was a thinly-veiled attempt to cover his tracks after Rothstein rejected Levin's last ditch efforts to persuade Rothstein to keep the Ponzi scheme going." In support, plaintiffs rely on an October 31, 2009, email from Preve to Rothstein stating that:

"We [Levin and Preve] understand that the shortage is *now 300m which is still manageable if we have your cooperation*. Let me know," to which Rothstein responds, "[t]hat is not the shortage ... that is the amount of money needed to give the investors back their money. I really just need to end it, Frank. It will make it easier for everyone." [emphasis added].

The attempt to try and "manage" the hole created now presumes that Levin and Preve had knowledge of a prior deficit and serves as an unwitting admission of their involvement in the perpetuation of the Ponzi scheme.

According to a March 18, 2010 article in the Daily Business Review by reporter Julie Kay, one of Rothstein's banks became concerned about money laundering by RRA. It was nearly $15,000,000 in wire transfers in July of 2008 that caused the concern. Then in May of 2009, Gibraltar Bank had suspicions and sent an email to Rothstein for clarifications. It asked for documentation and the purpose of the payments. It also asked for a confirming letter from RRA's CPA.

On March 17, 2010, the bankruptcy trustee took the deposition of Gary Berkowitz of RRA's accounting firm, Berenfeld. Berkowitz said in response to a question, he and his boss, Tracy Weintraub ... wrote Ansari to assure her the large deposits were "recorded as revenue on the books of the law firm and will be reflected as income on their tax return for 2008." The article indicates '… the accountants added, "This information was not audited by our firm, and we make no representation regarding the sufficiency of this information for any credit decision-making purposes."' Under questioning, Berkowitz revealed Rothstein asked the accountants to remove a line from the letter stating "we provide no proof of accuracy" and remove the word "verified" from the sentence "this information was not audited or verified by our firm."

Rothstein wrote Berkowitz: "Hey bro – need to see you this afternoon about sending a nebulous letter over to Gibraltar Bank about the fact that I am declaring certain funds as income to my firm … need the letter so I do not breach confidence on the settlement side. Love ya, me, me and me." That was classic Rothstein. The way he wrote and always hiding behind the confidentiality of his clients. The email ended with a joke: "Let's do this info over a cigar" and "How is the SEC … hehehehehe." They met at Starbuck according to the article.

In the deposition "Berkowitz repeatedly acknowledged making mistakes in approving financial reports that went to Rothstein's banks and in his firm preparing and signing off on tax returns without having solid knowledge of the source of Rothstein's deposits." He and his firm actually had major concerns since the increase in payroll cost could not be shown to be supported by increased business or even be afforded by the firm.

"Were you alarmed by the fact that the firm's income jumped $20 million from 2006 to 2007?" Scruggs asked. Berkowitz said he wasn't. On another matter he acknowledged that Rothstein attempted to convince him about a million dollar fee that was not credible. Berkowitz said. "I couldn't believe they would pay more than a million dollars to a law firm."

In life there will always be people looking to see what is in it for themselves or looking the other way when the situation calls for careful analysis. But appreciate the difference when neighbors are available on a moment's notice 24/7, and rush to analyze the needs of others, and then fill those needs because other people are important. The story I call "Hatzalah Bridges the Gap" is a life saver.

Hatzalah Bridges the Gap

February 14, 2010, was "Family Fun Day" for one of our local schools. The event was held several miles north of the community. Everyone was having a great time when, all of a sudden, a child had a seizure and his airway began closing. 9-1-1 was called. They were there in about five minutes – which is relatively fast – and fortunately the child was okay. But, what about those first five minutes? Those are long minutes when help is needed.

Fortunately, as one person was calling 9-1-1 another was calling the newly-established Hatzalah of Miami-Dade. Within seconds of the call, Hatzalah members Rabbi Yaakov Fried, Rabbi Chaim Glazer, and Zalmy Cohen were there to assist until fire rescue arrived. Shimshon Mindick arrived shortly thereafter.

Our local "Hatzalah" started operating on February 1, 2010, and began with a portion of North Miami Beach and Aventura. Members are now being recruited and trained for other local communities as well. Four Hatzalah members were in attendance at Family Fun Day. The theory of Hatzalah is that its members – all of whom are Florida-certified EMTs – generally live and work in the immediate community they serve, so they can often respond within three minutes of the call.

Hatzalah operates 24/7 and its members have responded to many life-threatening situations in just its first weeks of operation. An elderly man was injured and Joseph Dahan of Hatzalah was there in three minutes. When the local Fire Rescue arrived, Hatzalah turned the patient over in a stabilized condition. When a baby went into respiratory distress, Hatzalah's first member was there in three minutes, and a second one in four minutes. They were able to stabilize the baby before Fire Rescue arrived.

Hatzalah is the second call one should make; 9-1-1 is always first. Unlike in communities in other states, Hatzalah volunteers are not permitted under local law to provide emergency transport. Only official agencies (generally, county Fire Rescue) may provide ambulance services. Hatzalah is not a replacement for Fire Rescue, but is there to bridge the gap and provide vital services until Fire Rescue arrives. One patient responded that he could not imagine living in a community without Hatzalah. Now he doesn't have to.

Neighbors recognized that the Jewish community had unique challenges when it came to receiving emergency medical services. Language and customs were just two of the issues. Elderly Holocaust survivors often hesitated to call strangers. Less government revenues and more traffic congestion could result in delays. There were three options: complain, wait patiently, or bridge the gap. Bridging the gap is what many of my neighbors chose to do.

Thus, the formation of Hatzalah, an all-volunteer emergency medical service organization in our community. Neighborhood volunteers stepped forward to undergo a minimum of 280 hours of training, plus actual practice in local emergency rooms and ambulances. Thus far, twenty-five have become certified – and they are joined by ten volunteer dispatchers. All training costs, medical equipment, and supplies were paid for with donations from grateful community members – and from snowbirds who now have just another familiar service available to them. The service is 100 percent free and is available to anyone within the boundaries in which Hatzalah operates.

Hatzalah is a concept which is: people helping people – the antithesis of the type of behavior shown in the Rothstein second amended complaint. In Rothstein's world, the ideal was to take full advantage of anyone you could. In my community, the ideal is to give as much as you can of yourself and your services so that your friends and neighbors are cared for.

Chapter 17

What About the Plaintiffs?

We learn from history that we do not learn from history.

~Georg Wilhelm Hegel

W
HAT ROTHSTEIN DID in hatching his scheme and persuading others to go along with it is absolutely unforgivable. And, each defendant with personal knowledge of the scam deserves the same civil and criminal fate as Rothstein. But it's all of those "failing to exercise reasonable care" allegations in the second amended complaint against the defendants that shout out the question: Weren't the plaintiffs also asleep at the wheel? The plaintiffs were relying on all of the defendants and maintain that but for the defendants "failing to exercise reasonable care" they would not have lost their money. Wait a second. If it was so obvious that each defendant should have known, why didn't the plaintiffs know it was a scam? Shouldn't they have been suspicious?

When I was a young lawyer, Miami attorney Jerry Green gave me some great advice while I was considering taking a "difficult" client: "You make your money from the cases you turn down, not the cases you take," said Jerry.

There is a lot of truth to that. If you pass up a good case or a good opportunity, you will find another one. If you take a bad case or get involved with a bad situation, it can consume your time, stain your reputation, and drain your resources. It was good advice then and it is good advice now.

Though obtaining degrees and gaining experience is important, we must never forget to use our common sense. When evaluating these "investments," all we needed was the first two principles required for conducting any due diligence. The first principle is to rely on our own common sense and ask ourselves:

a. Does the investment seem plausible?

b. Does it pass the smell test?

c. Is there a reasonable correlation between the risk and the return?

If the answer to any of the sub-questions is "no," and the opportunity sounds too good to be true, then generally it will not be true and needs further investigation.

The second principle is "trust but verify" (Ronald Reagan's signature phrase). This is an essential part of conducting any due diligence. No one can be expected to buy something that cannot be verified in any manner, and those who do, do so at their peril. Redacted documents, inability to speak with the lawyers, inability to view the files, and inability to speak with the seller are all signs that trouble may be looming.

With those two principles in mind, let's look at the fabricated investments the plaintiffs listed in the initial lawsuit they believed they purchased from Rothstein's "clients" through [various] funds and decide if we think the investors "reasonably relied" on the statements of the defendants who did not have actual knowledge:

According to the second amended complaint, the first investment was a "$40,600,000.00 structured settlement, payable in four equal monthly installments, offered in exchange for a lump sum payment of $23,200,000 ...."

Not bad! The return on that "investment" was a whopping 322 percent per annum. That should have sounded off some bells and whistles to the plaintiffs, or at least raised a big red flag. After all, it was supposed to be as close to a risk-free investment as possible. The "investment" was to be guaranteed[12] by Rothstein, RRA and George G. Levin, the chief executive officer of [various funds], a person the plaintiffs were led to believe was worth more than $400,000,000.

Remember that the second amended complaint states that Levin had previously owned and operated GGL Industries, Inc. d/b/a Classic Motor Carriages, a company convicted of federal fraud charges. Why do the plaintiffs know that now? And why did they not know it then? If they did know it, why would they make an investment based on the word of someone who had operated a company that was convicted of federal fraud charges?

The plaintiffs believed, before making their investment, that all of the money they were expecting to receive was already being held in a segregated RRA trust account, irrevocably designated for them. The account was believed to require two signatures to withdraw money for their additional protection. That way one person alone could not misappropriate the money. How could the money have been irrevocably transferred into an account for the plaintiffs before the plaintiffs paid the lump sum purchase price for the settlement agreements? What if the plaintiffs changed their minds and the funds had already been placed in an irrevocable account for their benefit? That would have meant the investor was the only one who could receive the money even if he never invested. It was explained to us that a settlement agreement was not signed until an investor was identified. The investor only put up the money after the settlement agreement was funded by the wrongdoer.

The settlement agreement also had a code identifying the investor on page two of the settlement agreement. That would be entered before the settlement agreement was executed and only signed after

---

12 A guaranty, in legal terms, is a promise to pay someone if the person or entity who is supposed to pay does not do so.

the investor was identified and agreed to put up the money. What would happen if the investor did not pay the money he agreed to?

The plaintiffs believed there was an independent third-party verifier and one of the big four accounting firms involved in protecting their money. The independent third-party verifier and alleged major accounting firm were employed much like the other props, just to give the appearance that reviews and verification of authenticity were made by persons without loyalty to RRA or Rothstein.

The plaintiffs believed they were purchasing a "structured settlement." Structured settlements are funded by annuities[13] and, in most states, including Florida, require approval of a court to transfer them to someone else. Didn't the plaintiffs notice there was no annuity involved and there was no court approval? Most of the fabricated settlements Rothstein was peddling were not purported to be "structured settlements." They were confidential settlements of matters settled without a lawsuit being filed. It is likely that the opportunities being sold were characterized as settlements without a lawsuit being filed so that potential investors would not have the opportunity to inspect court files. If settlements were alleged to be made after suits were filed, a simple examination of the court files would have shown they did not exist. Also, the plaintiffs would have realized that a court had not approved the settlement.

After purchasing the first "investment," did the plaintiffs compare the settlement agreement with the template one in the Confidential Offering Memorandum? If they did, did they notice they were identical? My guess is that they were identical except for the size of the redacted names and the amounts and number of payments. If they noticed it, didn't that set off an alarm in their minds? Did they notice all of their settlement agreements were the same? Didn't they wonder why all of the various defense attorneys did not make a single change to the documents to protect their respective clients?

---

13 An annuity is a contract between the annuity owner and an insurance company. In return for the annuity owner's payment, the insurance company agrees to provide either a regular stream of income or a lump sum payout at some future time (generally, once the annuity owner retires or passes age 59 1/2).

Yes, Rothstein is a disgraceful scammer, but how did the plaintiffs not see it coming? And why do the plaintiffs believe that the defendants, many of whom had less business experience and training than the investors, were better prepared to protect them than they were themselves? When I mention "defendants," I am, of course, excluding any defendant named in this lawsuit with actual knowledge of the scam.

With all of the expected protection and guarantees in place, if the investments were real, the plaintiffs would be investing with a risk level close to putting money into a bank account. Why then were banks paying two percent and the first investment paying 322 percent? It just doesn't make sense! According to the second amended complaint, the plaintiff was not receiving all of the profit from the investment. The plaintiffs would have received the first fifteen percent, and the promoter the balance. Nonetheless, the plaintiffs needed to ask how the investment could yield 322 percent.

To show how absurd this was, let's start with a dollar. Everyone has a dollar. A dollar is nothing, you say. Well, if it were invested for twenty years at 322 percent, it would become something. At the end of twenty years it would amount to 187 billion dollars. Twenty years is a long time. How about fifteen years? You can turn your dollar into 54 million dollars. How about twelve years? You can exchange a dollar for 1.6 million dollars. Not bad, but still too long? How about five years to convert one dollar into $453? Instead of a dollar, why not start with $1,000? If you do, in five years that is $453,000.

Here is an example of a dollar growing at 322 percent:

End of year 1: $4.22
        2:      $13.59
        3. $43.75
        4:      $140.89
        5:      $453.67
        6:    $1,460.80
        7:    $4,703.79
        8: $15,146.19

You get the picture. By now, it should be clear that to make 322 percent or 200 percent or 100 percent, or even 50 percent, should alert one that there is a lot of risk. However, there is nothing wrong with risk. If the settlement investments were real but unfunded, and there was a substantial chance that the settlement or a large portion of it would be uncollectible, then a high return would be called for. The settlements collected would need to compensate for all of the settlements not collected. Investing in the early stages of experimental drugs, or in gold mines, or oil wells also pays a high return if the investment is successful, since it is unproven. As a rule of thumb, generally the lower the risk, the lower the return. The higher the risk, the greater the return. That is fundamental. The market is fairly efficient and returns will generally adjust based upon the perceived risk.

We also have to wonder what Scott was thinking. At 322 percent per annum, in five years, a dollar turns into $453. He was putting himself on quite a fast treadmill. How long could he have lasted at those numbers? Not long.

The initial plaintiffs in the first lawsuit made five other investments with Rothstein. These investments provided returns of 280 percent, 202 percent, and three at 322 percent. Two hundred and two percent is nothing to sneeze at but it seems almost insulting once you are receiving 322 percent. As a general rule, when a person makes an investment, that investment becomes the baseline for evaluating other investments, especially other nearly identical investments. Did the plaintiffs ask why such a large disparity in return existed when the risk was absolutely identical?

From a forensic accounting point of view, three factors are almost always found in every fraud, this one included: opportunity, pressure, and rationalization. Rothstein had an opportunity since he controlled his firm. He cleverly paid all of his attorneys a salary, rather than paying them based upon billable hours or paying them a share of profits, so that no one other than he and Rosenfeldt had a right or a reason to review the firm's financial records. Rosenfeldt trusted Rothstein implicitly so, with no controls in place, Scott had the ability to manipulate the financial records of the law firm without anyone noticing except those who were complicit with him.

The next element needed to commit a fraud is pressure. Rothstein was spending more in the operation of his firm than he was taking in. He also lived a lifestyle of almost unbelievable excess, spending like there was no tomorrow. That gave him the pressure needed to satisfy the second leg of the financial triangle.

Rationalization is the final component needed. Rothstein may have believed at one time that he would be able to pay the money back and rationalized that it was not stealing since he was going to return it. He may have convinced himself that the people from whom he was taking the money had obtained their money in an illegal or unethical manner or had plenty of it. Scott may have fooled himself into believing that he was creating jobs, helping charities, and doing other good things with the money that more than made up for the bad. Whatever it was, he was able to put his mind at ease by rationalizing that it was fine to take what wasn't his. With that, everything was in place for the fraud to exist.

By the end of October 2009, after the plaintiffs' money was invested, Rothstein and RRA began to default on the investors' settlement payments and the Ponzi scheme began to unravel.

On October 26, 2009, one of the plaintiffs spoke with Rothstein at the Bova restaurant who, in between martinis, admitted that he was "having a bad day." Rothstein was joined by a woman and his bodyguard, believed to be Joe Alu, who may have witnessed this exchange.

On October 27, 2009, broker Richard Pearson, who had invested $18,000,000 in the Ponzi scheme, confronted Rothstein, who was sitting with Frank Spinosa inside of the Bova restaurant. Pearson, in Spinosa's presence, demanded to know why he had not received two scheduled payments due to him the week prior. Rothstein attempted to defuse the situation, leaving Spinosa visibly shaken.

In the lawsuit, the plaintiffs charged the defendants with among

other things "committing conversion,[14] fraudulent misrepresenta-
tion,[15] negligent misrepresentation,[16] negligent supervision,[17] breach
of fiduciary duty, civil conspiracy; and aiding and abetting fraud,
conversion and breach of fiduciary duty." They asked the Court for
their approximately $120,000,000 investment money back with
interest, punitive damages, legal fees and more.

Our community has a large variety of ways in which people in
our community act for the benefit of other people without expecting
anything in return. The following story illustrates such selflessness.

Every *Simcha (celebration)* Is A Double *Simcha*

Mazel Tov (congratulations) was the phrase heard most often
throughout the evening as the bride and groom mingled through
the crowd. It was a beautiful wedding. The hall was magnificent.
The dance floor, as large as it was, was packed as the couple's friends
and family danced to the sounds of the most popular local band.
The flowers were plentiful and enhanced an already stunning affair.
The wedding ceremony was held outside under the light of a full
moon. The hors d'oeuvres were fit for a king and there seemed to be
an endless supply of them. Between the hors d'oeuvres and the deli-
cious buffet there was every delicacy one could desire. Nearby the
wine and liquor flowed for hours. Then came the appetizer, the soup,
the salad, the main course and, on top of that, the dessert.

As the hour drew late, the music stopped, the traditional blessings

---

14 Conversion is the civil law equivalent of the crime of theft. Civil conspiracy is the civil equivalent
of criminal conspiracy – that is, an agreement to do something that is illegal in civil law.

15 Fraud is an intentional false representation of a material (important) matter or fact – whether by
words or by conduct, by false or misleading allegations, or by concealment of what should have been
disclosed. It must deceive and must be intended to deceive another person so that the other person
will act upon it to his detriment. A fraudulent misrepresentation is a false statement of fact made by
a person who is aware that it is false. He makes the statement to induce another party to enter into a
contract and the other party does so as a result of the statement. The other party then suffers a loss.

16 Negligent misrepresentation is much the same thing except that the misrepresentation is not
intentional. It occurs when the defendant carelessly makes a statement of fact while having no
reasonable basis to believe it is true.

17 Negligent supervision occurs when an employer does not provide sufficient supervision to ensure
that employees comply with the employer's rules and regulations.

given after the wedding ended, the band packed up and the flowers were removed from the tables. Everyone at the affair had plenty to eat. But what about those who were not at the affair? Did they have plenty to eat? That was a question to which Pesach and Barbara Goodman, owners of Embassy Caterers, the caterer of this night's affair, knew the answer all too well. Pesach was aware that many of his neighbors could not afford to purchase adequate food for their families. Therefore, as the night's affair concluded, he asked the parents of the bride how much of the leftovers he could pack for the family to take home. Once the family took what it desired, Mr. Goodman mentioned that there were many families in the community who did not have the funds to put a good meal on their tables. He then asked, as he always asks the person whose affair it is, if they would like him to arrange for the leftovers to be distributed among families in need. The answer is always the same, "Absolutely."

Pesach does not know which families are in need and takes special precautions to be sure that they receive the food while it is still fresh and appetizing, without the recipient becoming known to him or to more people than necessary. After the wedding, and it is the same after other weddings, *bar mitzvahs*, *bat mitzvahs*, *shul* dinners, school dinners, and other parties, Pesach has his staff pack and preserve the remaining food so it can be distributed to those in need in a matter of just hours. At times Pesach will contact a neighbor who provides food on a regular basis to families in need, and he will arrange to park his catering truck at a designated location and families are invited to go to the truck and take what they need in an orderly manner, one at a time, so each person's dignity is preserved. There is no need for anyone to see or know who needs an extra hand during a difficult time.

For quite a while Pesach ordered sixty-four *challahs* every Thursday to give to a group of individuals who give away packages of food to families in need.

The other procedure Pesach employs is to deliver the remaining food to Yisrael Meir Cohen. Yisrael Meir repackages the food in family-size portions and keeps it in the refrigerators he purchased for this beautiful *mitzvah* (good deed) until he can deliver it to the families on his route. Yisrael Meir also goes to other caterers to pick up their leftovers so all remaining food can be used as a mitzvah.

Within my community, there are many people who generously take care of others either by giving of their time, resources, or money. One doesn't need to perform due diligence in order to determine the motivation but rather such selflessness is the norm for the people who live in my neighborhood.

Chapter 18

Charity is a Gift to the Giver

*Surplus wealth is a sacred trust which
its possessor is bound to administer in his
lifetime for the good of the community.*

~ANDREW CARNEGIE

BOVA PRIME, the restaurant of which Scott was part
owner, was located on Las Olas Boulevard in the heart
of Fort Lauderdale on the first floor of the same building
where RRA had its main office. It was a convenient
hangout for Scottie and his cronies. Even the Fort Lauderdale chief
of police, Frank Adderley, could be found there at least once a week.
Scottie held court at Bova Prime and was the center of attention. At
Bova, everyone knew who could make things happen, and the regulars knew how to give proper homage to their patron. Deal-making,
gossiping, and favor currying were on Bova's daily menu.

Now that Rothstein is in prison and no longer holding court
at Bova, certain blogs have become the source for information
and gossip about the Rothstein scandal. Although initially many
facts of the Rothstein saga were actually first revealed on various
blogs, very quickly the comments on the main blog covering the

Rothstein scandal disintegrated into a collection of hate filled and anti-Semitic grapevine rants and irrelevant stories and chat room babble. Quickly, those posting valuable comments departed and the quality of the posts dropped further. This is not uncommon where the privilege of speech is not tempered with personal responsibility or accountability.

Many of the comments on blogs relating to Rothstein's journey complimented Scott Rothstein for at least being charitable. Nothing could be further from the truth. Giving away someone else's money is not being charitable. Giving charity is a privilege one can only avail oneself of with one's own money. Even when giving charity with one's own money, there are different levels of giving with the highest level being helping a person become independent.

Rabbi Chaim Soloveitchik of Brisk used to say, "Both the *bal habayis* [head of the household] and the cat seek to eliminate any mice in the house but there is a vast difference between them. The human wants to get rid of all mice forever; the cat wants only to eat a specific mouse now, with the hope of finding another mouse later. By the same token, there are two different ways of giving *tzedakah* [charity] – in order to eliminate another's need or, on the other hand, for one's own gratification. There are some people who receive such enjoyment in giving *tzedakah* that they would be devastated if poverty were totally eliminated."[18]

America is a great country. There is no limit to what a person can legally earn. All one has to do is develop skills that are in demand and not easily replaced. Even better, a person's money can work harder than the person himself. Making a major discovery or invention, or investing in a company that does either one can lead to earning more money than a person can spend in a few lifetimes. But then what? What is the purpose of money? Money is a tool. Money allows us to purchase many of the things we want or need. Every one of us has different situations, challenges, and desires in life, so our wants and

---

18 *Words of Wisdom, Words of Wit* by Shmuel Himelstein, Mesorah Publications, Ltd., as part of the Artscroll series.1993. Page 32.

needs are dissimilar. As a result, the amounts of money we need to live our lives in the manner we choose and to retire as we please are also different.

But what about that extra money, the money that exists beyond what we calculate we will ever need or use, after establishing a comfortable cushion for inflation, downturns in the economy, and errors? Since money is a tool, it would be like having thousands of screwdrivers when just a few will serve the same purpose.

At the end of our lives we cannot take money with us. Even if we could, money is a currency for this world. In the next world, money may just be scrap paper. But what if our deeds from this world are the currency of the next world? What if how we live our lives in this world has a value in this world and in the next world? What if we could perfect this world by using our excess money and even a portion of our earnings that we do not deem "extra" to help others?

So many of us live as if life were a board game in which the rules provide that the winner is the one with all the money and property, and our opponents are left bankrupt. In life, benevolence plays an important function in perfecting the world. The rules of a good life require us to help others be able to provide for themselves.

Giving back to society has many benefits. First, and most importantly, it helps others. We can choose to help society in the way we deem best. After all, we received the "extra money" to make a meaningful difference toward making the world better. It is money we certainly would not want to waste since there are so many people and causes that need help. The power to make a difference is in our hands and our bank accounts. How great it is that we can make the choice of where and how we want to make that difference. G-d could send the money directly to where it is needed, but He gives us the chance to perfect the world by using the extra money, and even money that is not extra but that we put aside, so we can help others. It is a privilege, not a burden.

None of us can solve all of the world's problems but we can each help out in some way. By helping out early, we can help out when the solution is small. When we do not intervene early and prevent a problem, the cost in time and money to correct it later is much greater. Regardless of the amount, when we are helping, we are perfecting the world. Just imagine if we all directed our "surplus" cash to help others. The cumulative effect would be tremendous. Even helping just one person changes that person's world in a meaningful way; but for the giver, the benefit is immeasurable. The giver receives a feeling of inner satisfaction that comes from helping others and knowing he has made a difference. As Ralph Waldo Emerson said, "It is one of the most beautiful compensations of this life that no man can sincerely try to help another without helping himself."

Rav Yerucham Levovitz explained: G-d did not invent the *mitzvos* [plural of *mitzvah*] of charity and loving-kindness because He saw that there were poor people in the world who needed help. Rather, He created poor people so that there would be an opportunity for mankind to fulfill the *mitzvah* of charity. A world without kindness is inconceivable, for the very purpose of creation is to instill in mankind the divine attributes of compassion and benevolence.[19] Rabbi Feuer quotes his *Rebbe* (Spiritual Teacher), *Rav* Mordechai Gifter, who enlightened him that the, "Greek philosopher Plato, in his classic work, *The Republic*, attempts to design the perfect economic and social system – Eutopia. ("Eu" is a Greek prefix meaning "good.") At first Plato sees great merit in a socialistic system where all wealth is shared equally; but ultimately, he rejects such a scheme, because it would obviate the opportunity for man to exercise philanthropy by giving charity."

Rabbi Tzvi Eliyohu Meir Schmelczer, head of the North Miami Beach Community Kollel, offered further proof of the importance of charity to the giver. *Rav* Schmelczer points out that before the giving of the *Torah* at Sinai, the leaders of the Jewish people inspired each person to contribute what they could afford to the building of

---

19 "The Uneven Distribution of Wealth," *Tehillim Treasury* by Rabbi Avrohom Chaim Feuer, Mesorah Publications, Ltd., as part of the Artscroll Series, 1993." Page 79.

the Tabernacle. The leaders immediately committed to contribute any deficit no matter how great. This, Rabbi Schmelczer suggests, is the dream of every fundraiser. Yet, when the *Torah* records the incident, it does so in a negative fashion. Our rabbis point out, more is expected of leaders and on their level, those leaders failed to rise to the challenge. He notes that although they inspired the people and committed to make up the shortfall, they, the leaders, also should have immediately contributed money themselves since the purpose of charity is to help the giver by developing his character. If that was not the case, G-d would take care of the poor and the worthy causes Himself.

On Tuesdays at lunchtime, for several years, I have had the privilege of attending a *Torah* class given by Rabbi Moshe Gruenstein, the Rabbi of Young Israel of Bal Harbour, Florida. A few years ago, Rabbi Gruenstein shared a beautiful insight of The Vilna Gaon's disciple, Chaim of Valozhin, regarding *Rosh Hashanah* (The Jewish New Year). Rabbi Gruenstein said in the name of Chaim Valozhin that on *Rosh Hashanah* G-d judges the living and the dead. What does this mean? I understand judging the living and even judging a person who died during the year. Certainly he did good things and bad things even in a short year. But why judge a person several years after he passed away? While he was alive he could do great things and horrible things, but what can a dead person do?

Rav Chaim Valozhin brilliantly explains that what a person does during his lifetime is what a person can be judged for during his lifetime. But he can also be judged for everything others did because of his influence. In other words, if a person helped someone out and as a result that person did great things, both the person that did the great things gets credit and so does the person who influenced him. The same goes for charity. If we give charity and it helps people, and as a result the beneficiaries are able to do acts of kindness or give charity themselves, then we get credit as well. Now it is easy to understand why the departed need to be judged every year. Their actions while alive are paying dividends even after they leave this world!

Imagine giving charity to support an institution that helps a tremendous number of people. When we sleep we will be accruing benefits and, when we leave the world, we will still be accruing rewards. Now imagine that our conduct influences others. Chaim Valozhin articulated the greatest multilevel accounting system long before Amway was even a thought. When we give charity, we can help someone who needs help, we can enjoy the great feeling that goes along with helping others and while we sleep and when we enter the World of Truth, we are still receiving benefits.

According to the November 4, 2009, article on *The Daily Pulp*, written by Bob Norman, after a Rothstein investor realized nearly $100,000,000 of his family's money was invested in Rothstein's Ponzi scheme, he said, "It was an amount I wish I'd given to charity instead of that investment. It won't change my lifestyle that much, but it was a nice sum …. I will still eat out at a restaurant every night; this is just something I need to get through."

I hope the investor gets his money back. If he does not, I hope he earns it again so that he can get his wish. Too bad he did not have the idea of giving that money to charity before it made its way to the master of deception. Many people come to the same conclusion after losing their money. How many people have said, "When I make a million dollars, I'll give a large donation to charity?" Only they change it to the next million after earning the first.

In addition to the reasons we have discussed – to eliminate another's need, for our own gratification, to help to perfect the world, to influence others, to be judged after we are gone by our positive influence on others while we were alive there is still another reason to help. For selfish reasons, one can help out in ways that help the many children falling through the cracks of society. These children gravitate to gangs because they do not find acceptance elsewhere. There are children who do not have the basic skills to succeed in school and do not have parents, tutors or mentors to help them. In time, they grow up without the confidence or ability to earn a meaningful living and quickly discover or continue a life of crime. If enough people contributed enough time and money to assist youth early on, we could actually see a reduction in the cost of goods as a result of fewer thefts in stores. We could also see a reduction in the cost of law enforcement. We would also be able to walk down the street with a lower likelyhood of becoming a victim of crime.

By taking the opportunity to help others, we will see that we are perfecting the world little by little. The cumulative effect of so many more people helping will make a meaningful difference. It will also lead to inspiring more people to help others. The following story is a fine illustration of such ideals.

Amazing Abe

For Passover, Dr. Abe Chames would carefully calculate what it cost to take his family of five to a fancy hotel including airfare and the works. Once he knew the full cost, instead of going to the hotel, Abe would purchase $50 and $100 food vouchers from Publix super-market with the same amount of money. Abe rationalized that food for Passover is very expensive and while it is a nice holiday to go away and leave the cooking to the chef at the hotel, but he did not want to go to a hotel for Passover when so many people could not even afford food for the holiday. Upon returning from Publix, Abe divided the thousands of dollars of vouchers into dozens of enve-lopes and then, so no one knew he was involved, had someone give the envelopes anonymously to neighbors and rabbis who were in need.

Publix vouchers were not the only vouchers Abe bought. He always had a supply of vouchers to Disney World on hand. Abe and his family loved their trips to Disney World, but why in the world would he need so many vouchers? Simple: he wanted every child to have the full Disney experience, one with all the trim-mings. Not everyone could afford such a trip, so Abe gave families vouchers to Disney World. Why then did he not just give them cash? Because many of the families he gave vouchers to could not ratio-nalize spending money on Disney World when they needed money for their mortgage, electric bill, and even shoes. Abe felt they still needed a day or two to forget their worries and give their kids the time of their life. If he gave them cash, they would undoubtedly spend part on entrance fees and save most of the money for their ongoing living expenses. Abe discovered that "Disney Dollars" could not be redeemed for cash. Therefore, each recipient was "forced" to spend every dollar and enjoy the experience to the fullest.

Abe's kindness came in many forms. Once, Abe saw a teacher at a Jewish private school in my community with worn-out shoes. He did not want to embarrass this person but he did want to see him receive the necessary money to get new shoes or pay other urgent expenses. He needed to figure out a way to get him and other teachers extra money without destroying their dignity. He was at a loss as to what he should do. Abe's rabbi had a great idea. His rabbi told him that businesses give holiday bonuses. He could do the same and the recipients would not feel like they were receiving charity. They would feel appreciated and be most grateful. Abe did just that but he did it in a way that made it look like the money came from the parents of many students.

On December 6, 2008, Abe Chames unexpectedly died and the world lost a tremendous person who was constantly involved in doing acts of kindness and charity. These few examples of Abe's inventive ways to enhance the lives of others give a mere glimpse of the enormity of the void that exists after his untimely death.

Abe loved that so much of his giving was done anonymously and the reward he received was the joy of knowing that he was helping so many people without recognition. He gave freely from the funds he had worked hard to accumulate and yet never felt that he was any poorer even while giving away tremendous sums of his own money.

Chapter 19

A Little Help
is Often a Big Help

*There is no better exercise
for your heart than reaching down
and helping to lift someone up.*

~Bernard Meltzer

ROTHSTEIN MADE A PRACTICE of enticing decent people and bringing them down to his level. He continually brought people to their lowest common denominator. It is almost as if Scottie liked to entangle everyone around him into his web of corruption. Maybe he felt that way no one could turn him in, since they broke the law as well. Maybe he knew that one day he would be caught and he wanted to make sure there were people he could turn in, in exchange for a lighter sentence. On December 1, 2009, as Scottie Rothstein stood before the federal magistrate, his collateral damage was completed even though those other individuals were not yet charged. The charges were only against Scott Rothstein at that point, but they mentioned that there were other "known and unknown co-conspirators."

When we are around a person like Scott we need to ask ourselves, "What could we have done when he was a little off-course, when he needed a little help, when he was moving in the wrong direction?

What could we have done to help him get back on track?" The time, energy and money invested back then might have prevented this tragedy. If he could not have been helped, at least others could have been protected from him.

As the special agent in charge of the FBI's Miami office, John V. Gillies, said, "This does not appear to be a one-man job." There will likely be many individuals indicted for criminal activity, whether for participating in the fraud, violating the campaign fundraising laws, or other criminal activity. Many of the people surrounding Scott were decent people, not planning to get involved in crime, happy with themselves, happy earning a decent living, and happy with the home they lived in and the car they drove.

Rabbi Shapiro says that from the words *matza* and *chametz* we receive an insight into how problems occur. The two words in Hebrew each have two of the same letters just in a different order. The remaining letter of each word is different and at that there is only a small difference. *Matza* (unleavened bread) which is kosher during Passover has a *Hay* ה. *Chametz* (bread) which is not kosher during Passover has a *Ches* ח. The only difference between the Hebrew letters is a small line. The difference between kosher and unkosher, acceptable and unacceptable, and right and wrong is also very small – that is how it all starts. People are influenced by the people around them. Little by little, one bad judgment after another, a person can go from being a decent law-abiding citizen to becoming an accomplice and co-conspirator in a major crime. Those decent people I am speaking of certainly had free will and made choices on their own. But those bad choices just show us the importance of surrounding ourselves with the proper kind of friends, the proper kind of co-workers, the proper kind of neighbors, and even the proper kind of spouse. We need to walk away from this tragedy and grow from it and be better people from it. We need to help one another stay on the right path.

Many of the people who were closest to Rothstein became like him to some degree. Some may have doctored up documents to pass them off as true. Some may have stolen money. Some may have ignored the campaign contribution laws. Others may have seen conduct that didn't make sense and ignored it because they were deriving benefits from it. It was all too good to let the obvious be stopped. Fred Grimm cleverly pointed out in his November 4, 2009, column in the *Miami Herald* that they needed to ignore obvious fundamental flaws since "… they were in the same fix as the fellow in the old Woody Allen joke whose brother thought he was a chicken. He knew his brother was insane but he needed the eggs."

Rabbi Shapiro speaks of situations where people needed a little help by comparing the Hebrew words נְשַׁמָה (*neshuma*) and נְשָׁמָה (*neshama*). The words look the same and sound nearly the same but they are very different. In Hebrew the vowels are below the letters. Look at the vowel under the second letter of each word. In the first word, the vowel is called a *patach*. It looks like a minus sign (–). The definition of that word is "desolate or void." The second word has a vowel called a *kamatz* (T) under it. It looks like a "T." It is the same sign as under the first word except it also has a line going down. It has a little support. The definition of the second word is "soul" or "life." Rabbi Shapiro says so powerfully, as only he can say, "When you have a situation that is desolate or there is a void, if you give it a little support, just a little support, then you have a soul. Then you have life. It is that small amount of effort we need to give to a person in need that can help a person fill a void and give him life."

That is what it is to live with one's heart on the right side. We need to recognize these situations and intervene early. We can make a real difference.

A neighbor mentioned to me what an impact a sentence in a card my wife wrote made on his son. Leah wrote a nice card and attached it to a gift as a *bar mitzvah* present. My wife was unaware that the young man was going through a period where he lacked self-confidence. Leah always has a kind word to say about everyone and was impressed by the beautiful speech the *bar mitzvah* boy delivered so she mentioned in the card that she sees beautiful leadership qualities in him. That is all it took. His father said the young man began to reevaluate his assessment of himself in a much more positive light. Sometimes it is as simple as a kind word that makes that difference. Since a person does not generally walk around with a sign on his forehead saying when he needs help or describing the help he needs, it is a good practice to be in the habit of always finding a reason to say a kind word and doing it in a genuine way.

In our community, people are doing what they can to give a helping hand to lift people up. The two stories I am sharing are about a person in my community. In fact, it is a person in my home, our eldest daughter, Nechama. *Nechama* means "comfort." We named our eldest daughter Nechama with the hope that she would be a source of comfort to others and I think from these stories it seems the name was well-chosen. The stories show the power of a thought and a prayer.

I Feel Your Pain

As *Shabbos* ended, it was enthusiastically proclaimed that the illness of a teacher of Nechama's was in remission. His Rabbi informed him he can recite a prayer that is said when a person survives a dangerous situation. There was no longer a need to pray for his recovery. That was great news and I ran home to recite *Havdalah* for my family (the benediction declaring the difference between the holy *Shabbos* and the rest of the week) and share the news with my family. After *Havdalah*, I said, "Nechama's teacher no longer needs our prayers."

As I made the statement, my daughter Nechama said nonchalantly, "Tonight I can sleep on a pillow."

"What?" I asked. "I do not get the connection."

"No, nothing," Nechama said as she walked toward her room.

Her sisters quickly explained to Leah and me that when her teacher had been diagnosed with a terrible disease, Nechama lay in bed thinking to herself how difficult it must be for her teacher to fall asleep. Then she thought how quickly she falls asleep and decided she needed to make some changes. Nechama thought to herself,

How can I just go to sleep while my teacher is suffering so? I need to pray for him and I need to feel his pain so I can properly pray for him.

Right then and there Nechama resolved that she would sleep without a pillow until her teacher recovered. After discussions with her three younger sisters, Nechama decided *Shabbos* and holidays would be the only exceptions. As Nechama tossed and turned in bed each night she could surely relate to the discomfort of her teacher and pray for his recovery with a full heart. When I mentioned this story to Nechama's teacher, his eyes began to tear up. I had to walk away. He was speechless and began to cry. He could not believe that, for over a year, his pain was Nechama's pain. An hour later he came by to explain to me the unparalleled strength and comfort Nechama's compassion provided him.

Eleven years before, when Nechama was about eight years old, I remember Nechama answering the phone. "It is *Howard*," she said. Howard was a neighbor that seemed to be a magnet for bad luck. Howard explained to me that he was two months behind on his rent and needed $1,000 to catch up. I offered him $200 toward the money he needed and he was offended.

"Two hundred dollars will not solve my predicament," he explained.

I thought it would get him a good way there and other neighbors would surely help.

"It was all or nothing," he said. Neither of us budged and I let Howard know the money was there if he changed his mind.

When I hung up Nechama asked me why I did not help Howard.

"Nechama," I said, "I tried to but he would not take the assistance I was offering."

Nechama said, "*Abba* (father), didn't you hear his voice? He was depressed. Why don't you just give him what he asked for?"

That amount was more than I usually give to a person asking for a little help but less than I would give to family. I tried to explain how many people a week come asking for help and how much $200 was, all to no avail.

Not understanding my failure to adequately assist Howard, Nechama asked if I was unwilling to help Howard, could we at least invite him over for *Shabbos* lunch and let him sit at my place at the table?

To that I said, "Sure" but I did not understand how that was a solution. While I disagreed with giving him the full $1,000, I did understand how Howard would find it helpful and how it would make sense to Nechama as well.

Nechama said, "*Abba*, don't you get it? If you do not want to help Howard, let him come over for *Shabbos* and sit in your chair. That way he will feel like a king and if he feels like a king for *Shabbos* and he is not depressed anymore, he will not need your money. He can solve his own problems."

Wow, was Nechama right! It was just like the story she heard from Rabbi Zev Leff a few years prior when she was five years old. Rabbi Leff was in town and Nechama sat on my lap when Leah and I went to hear Rabbi Leff speak. As we walked out Nechama asked me my favorite part and proceeded to tell me hers. I was amazed. We had brought Nechama and our son Yaacov with us because we did not have a babysitter. We did not expect a five-year-old to understand the lecture.

Nechama said her favorite part was when Rabbi Leff said a father was trying to read the newspaper and his daughter kept asking him questions. He wanted twenty minutes of quiet so he opened a magazine and saw a map of the world. He ripped it in many pieces and gave it to his daughter. He said, "Here is a puzzle of a map of the world. Try putting it together."

He figured that should buy him his twenty minutes, and maybe a lot more. Amazingly, five minutes later his daughter had the map together. The father asked his daughter how she did it so fast. She said on the back of the map was a picture of a person and when you put the person together, the whole world comes together.

How true that is! That is just what Nechama understood about Howard as well. If he could just feel like a person again, he could solve his own problems. He, in fact, found a way to bring his rent current without coming back to me. If we look at life with these goals in mind, we will be picking up the pieces from full-blown tragedies much less often.

A kind word is so powerful; it can change the world for a person when delivered in the time of need and with sincerity. Since frequently we do not know how badly a person needs to be shown compassion, we should err on the side of making it our habit.

Just as one self-absorbed person – the Rothsteins of the world – can lower the morale of others, so a person who puts others first can inspire others. This is evident in the story I call "One Person Can Make a Difference. That Person Can Be You. This Time It Was Sarah Palgon."

One Person Can Make A Difference. That Person Can Be You. This Time It Was Sarah Palgon.

All it takes is one person. One person to keep you on the right road, one person to inspire you to be the best you can be, one person to make you believe that you have what it takes to change the world. For *Maya*, a teenage girl, that one person was Mrs. Sarah Palgon of North Miami Beach, Florida.

Mrs. Palgon was Maya's teacher in middle school, a crucial time in the development of a teenage girl. As Maya's Judaic Studies teacher, Sarah Palgon answered every question and concern with thoughtfulness and respect. Unlike some teachers, Mrs. Palgon did not patronize any idea. She brought a whole new atmosphere into that cramped room, where learning was now a blessing and learning Torah was essential to life.

Later, as a public high school student, Maya remained devoutly religious, keeping kosher and meticulously observing *Shabbos* even when those around her were not. Throughout it all, Maya always thought to herself, "What would Mrs. Palgon do?"

By following this train of thought, she was always guided to do the right thing. As a high school senior, this student, number two in her class with outstanding SAT scores, had the opportunity to consider the Ivy League route. But there was no doubt in Maya's mind where the true Ivy League was. It was Stern College, the college Mrs. Palgon had attended. Now a college junior, Maya has excelled in her studies and is interning for a U. S. senator. Her major? Judaic Studies, of course! Mrs. Palgon has made such a difference in many people's lives. What an amazing *neshama* (soul) she is!

Mrs. Sarah Palgon is currently a teacher at Toras Emes Elementary school in North Miami Beach, Florida. Mrs. Palgon is known to not be able to sleep well at night when one of her students is not happy, or not doing well. Her commitment to her students has become legendary.

Mrs. Palgon's husband is no different. Rabbi Ephraim Palgon is the principal of our community's middle school. Years back he was my son's sixth grade teacher. Our son needed a little extra help with learning *Gemara*.[20] My wife, Leah, called Rabbi Palgon and asked if he could recommend a tutor. His answer was, "It is better if a father can teach his son. Please have Alan call me. I would like to learn an hour a week with Alan so that he can have the pleasure of learning together with Yaacov."

For the next year and a half, I was at the Palgon home every Tuesday night at eight P.M. It was a tremendous opportunity for me to learn directly with Rabbi Palgon, one on one. But every evening as I left, Rabbi Palgon thanked me for taking the time to learn with him. He said, "You have no idea how your learning with me and asking your questions helps me better prepare to teach my students. I really appreciate it."

---

20 The *Gemara* is commentaries on the *Mishnah*, which in turn is the compilation and writing down of the formerly oral part of the Torah. The *Gemara* and the *Mishnah* are written in Aramaic and together are called the *Talmud*, and were completed in the 5th century C.E.

These role models are the people that influence the people in my community. They are leaders whose "power" stems from their core values and beliefs. They give to the community with all their heart, understanding the grave responsibility they have as leaders.

Chapter 20

Ending the Entitlement Society

The road to Easy Street goes through the sewer.

~JOHN MADDEN

D ECEMBER 1, 2009. The rumors from the night before were rampant that Scott Rothstein was turning himself in or being arrested in the morning. At 7:45 A.M. indeed the FBI arrived to pick up Scottie Rothstein. After being processed he was brought into the federal courthouse in Broward County and presented with the charges against him. It was important that he be arrested so that the message was made clear to the public that Rothstein's conduct was reprehensible and would not be tolerated.

On that day, Rothstein's bankrupt philosophy needed to be arrested as well. This is the philosophy we all came to witness long before Rothstein entered the scene and some of us subscribed to in one way or another; that is, that we get something for nothing, the "entitlement society." Some thought they could buy respect, reputation, and awards. Back in the day one used to earn money, respect, and a reputation. Now some feel entitled to it or want to buy it. We need to return to the day when such things were earned.

Even though Rothstein needed to be arrested, at the same time, I could not help but have sympathy for the poor, self-deluded man, thinking of how he ruined his own life and those of many people around him. His grandmother believed in him and even used her life savings to put him through college and law school. Say what you like about Scottie, but he did have talent. For many years he represented his clients diligently and lived a normal, low-key life. Scott was an accomplished singer. He held a respectable position as an attorney. He obviously wasn't happy, though. However the path he took from that point on until his arrest certainly couldn't have made him any happier. He may have had the appearance to others of having good fortune, and even many may have thought he was the embodiment of success, but he was the epitome of excess. He had a need to look successful perhaps not only to pull off the scheme but so that people would think he was someone. He always wanted to be someone and must have felt like he was not. To quote Lily Tomlin: "I have always wanted to be somebody, but I see now I should have been more specific." Perhaps Scott, too, should have been more specific about what he wanted.

We live in a society where the notion of entitlement runs rampant. Too often, a person no longer saves for what he wants nor has the ability to make choices. He wants everything and has to have it. In fact, the word "wants" became synonymous with "needs." Rabbi Shapiro points to modern technology. He says everything has one thing in common; it's the "I." Everybody is buying the iPhone, iPod, iPad and iTunes. Everything has the same goal in mind; it's all about what "I" can get out of it. Once my Rabbi joked that Nintendo finally got it right and created a little unity in the world because Nintendo was bright enough to create the Wii, but he said even Nintendo blew it because it spelled it W-i-i.

Interestingly, when the rabbis of the Great Assembly initialed the Jewish prayer book 2,300 years ago, they were well aware of the dangers of a society focused on the "I." The first words a Jew utters in the morning upon awakening are words of gratitude to his Creator.

What a way to start off the day with an attitude of gratitude. But the prayer is grammatically incorrect. It should say "I thank G-d for ...." But the rabbis said, the first word in the morning cannot be "I" and so in Hebrew the "thank you" comes before the "I" as the first words in the first prayer even though it is grammatically incorrect.

Receiving entitlements when a person is capable of working provides an empty feeling since it lacks sacrifice, passion, and commitment. For those reasons, it doesn't work. A person deprives himself of the feeling of accomplishment when he tries to receive without effort that which must be earned. Addicting people who are capable of working to welfare and other handouts hurts the recipients and the country. It looks good in the short term but over the long haul it robs people of their ambition, desire, and self-confidence.

Welfare, food stamps, Section Eight housing vouchers, Medicaid, and similar programs are great for people who try their hardest and cannot earn enough to live without the extra governmental help. However, we should never look at such programs as something to which we are entitled or something we strive to one day obtain unless there is no better choice. Instead, we should strive to be self-sufficient and be in a position to help others in need. We should plan to obtain an education in a profession, trade or field that is well-suited for our talents and our interests and one that generally pays the type of salary that is, at a minimum, greater than what we expect our lifestyle will cost.

If we want our children to succeed we need to be proper role models from before they are born, but at least from today forward. It is never too late. We need to give our children encouragement and opportunities to succeed. We need to match the way they are taught to the way they learn. If they need additional help we need to be there to assist them and to guide them, but not to do the work for them. If we do not have the skills to help, hiring a capable tutor is the next best thing. Children need to understand that the harder they work as children to master skills, the easier they will have it as adults. The time to study for tests is not the night before tests; it's every day after class. Children need to outline what they learn and review it each day so on the day of their tests they are well prepared. At the same time, children should not be under so much pressure that they either do not enjoy school, do not have time for school activities or they are so nervous they end up getting an ulcer. None of these results are acceptable.

I was told by a friend that her husband's ninth-grade teacher said that the way to do well on the SAT is to "spend an hour a day reading the *New York Times*. If one doesn't like reading the paper, then read something else, even comic books." Those parents got their two daughters to buy into that philosophy and they each got a perfect score on the critical reading and writing sections of the SAT. Every child should be reading an hour a day from as young an age as they are able. And when children see their parents reading a book, a newspaper, or a magazine instead of watching television or sitting at the computer, then the children learn from their parents' example.

Almost everyone can improve his situation if he so desires. He just has to want it badly enough. Most important is having a meaningful goal, a can-do attitude and the willingness to pursue the goal until it is achieved.

Making one good choice after another is the start of living on the right path. Surrounding oneself with appropriate friends, co-workers, and clients/customers is also important. Living, working, and spending time in suitable environments is a necessity. Grounding oneself in an ethical system and staying infused with ethical values is also a requirement. But still, as we see from the following study, "The Dishonesty of Honest People," that is not enough. There is another ingredient needed.

Nina Mazar, On Amir, and Dan Ariely conducted experiments and presented their findings in a paper called "The Dishonesty of Honest People: A Theory of Self-Concept Maintenance." (2008) A series of tests were administered for which the participants were compensated based upon performance. All the tests were simple math tests consisting of twenty questions, but the participants were given only enough time (four-to-five minutes) to correctly answer about three questions.

In one experiment, the members of the first group were required to turn their tests in and the experimenter graded it. That group did not have the opportunity to cheat. On average, those test takers answered 3.1 questions right. The second group took the same test, and each person graded his own test and then merely told the experimenter how many were correct. The average number reported correct was 5.5 per participant. The third group took the same test but, before the test, they were asked to sign a statement at the top that read "I understand that this short survey falls under the MIT [Yale] honor code." That group also self-graded their tests and told the experimenter the number of questions they each answered correctly. The average number of questions answered correct, 3.

Based upon this and many other experiments they conducted, the experimenters'deduced that in general, people will cheat whenever the opportunity to do so exists. The exception is when a person is given a moral reminder close in time to the temptation. The experimenters other research demonstrated that most people consider themselves honest. Therefore, a person will only cheat if doing so will allow him to still consider himself honest. It is as if a person who views himself as honest has a conscience that protects him from dishonest activities when his conscience is engaged. The trouble is one's sense of right and wrong seems to generally be disengaged and once in place remains that way for a limited period of time.

One way a person's principles are activated is when he is confronted with a dishonest activity that he cannot easily rationalize as honest, such as committing an armed robbery. The second method to trigger the conscience is by a moral reminder just before the time of enticement. That reminder can be the signing of an honor code or as Mazar, Amir, and Ariely found in another experiment, the writing down of as many of the Ten Commandments as one could remember just before taking the test.

Further studies by the same group proved that the further removed the reward was from cash, the greater the degree a person will cheat. In a study they found when rather than cash for each correct answer, the participant received a token that he immediately handed to the next experimenter for conversion to cash, scores on the same test went up to 9.4 correct with 3.5 for the control group (those that did not have the opportunity to cheat) and 6.2 from the group with an equal opportunity to cheat but receiving cash for correct answers rather than tokens.

Sixteen hundred years ago, *Rav* Nachman's mother understood what the experiments confirmed. In the fifth century, *Rav* Nachman bar Yitzchak's mother was told by an astrologer that her son would grow up to be a thief. At the time it was the custom for Jewish men, but not Jewish children, to cover their heads. Nevertheless, *Rav* Nachman's mother recognized that if a person is predisposed to certain behavior, he must work harder to channel his conduct in an appropriate fashion and pray for divine assistance. She instructed him: "My son, cover your head completely, [as a reminder that G-d is above] so that you will fear G-d, and always pray for His mercy, so that you should not be overcome by your evil impulses."

The *Bavli Gemora* on page 156b in *Tractate Shabbos*, records that one day, *Rav* Nachman sat studying under a palm tree and his head covering fell off. Thereupon he looked up and saw dates in the tree and his evil inclination overpowered him and he ate the dates that belonged to someone else.

After that, *Rav* Nachman understood why his mother admonished him to cover his head and pray for mercy. *Rav* Nachman was so diligent in working on himself to overcome his predisposition that he went on to become one of the chief scholars of his generation. He was known to have sterling character.

Rav Salanter understood the necessity of being constantly engaged in the study of ethics. In the 1800s, *Rav* Yisroel Salanter was the father of the religious self-improvement (mussar) movement. He was among the greatest scholars of his time and stressed the importance of ethical behavior. Rabbi Akiva Zweig mentioned to me a story he heard from his father, Rabbi Yochanon Zwieg, the dean of the Talmudic University of Miami Beach. Rabbi Akiva Zweig says that he was told *Rav* Salanter said if he were in a room filled with diamonds and could take enough diamonds for his financial security and that of his children and grandchildren without anyone ever knowing what he did, he would take them.

It is said of his student, *Rav* Simcha Zissel Brodie, that he was not sure what he would do. About *Rav* Brodie's student, *Rav* Yerucham Levovitz, it is claimed that he would definitely not steal. Then *Rav* Yerucham Levovitz explains that *Rav* Salanter knew who he was, *Rav* Brodie was not sure who he was, and *Rav* Levovitz himself was so delusional as to think he knew who he was.

It is inconceivable that *Rav* Salanter would do such a thing. It must be that when he referred to himself, he meant "men in general" and was pointing out how powerful the urge is and how vulnerable men are to being lured into conduct that is inappropriate. The only other possiblity is that *Rav* Salanter, like *Rav* Nachman in the previous story appreciated his predisposition and was speaking about what he would do if he did not work on his character day and night and if he did not realize the great punishment from Heaven for such deviant conduct and such reward for perfecting one's character. *Rav* Salanter understood what the experimenters recently discovered about the dishonesty of honest people and the need to engage one's conscious by constantly learning about ethical behavior on a daily basis. *Rav* Salanter understood the danger of being enticed and the need to keep far away from such tempting situations.

The experiments and the stories confirm that we must constantly make good choices, surround ourselves with good people, work on ourselves daily, and pray for divine assistance, to have a fighting chance to be the best person we are capable of being and to avoid succumbing to wickedness disguised as opportunity as we reach each fork in the road of our life.

As a teenager, my former neighbor Israel Gurfinkel saw firsthand his friends sacrifice everything they had, including their lives, for the freedom and safety of others. My final story, "In My Mind" comes with a blessing that a great rabbi, The Steipler Goan, gave to a young soldier returning to war.

In My Mind Reverberates the Blessing The Steipler Gave to a Young Soldier Returning to War

Over a quarter century ago, Israel Gurfinkel fought in the first Lebanon War in Israel. His grandfather had been a student at the famous Novardok *Yeshiva* with Rabbi Yaakov Yisrael Kanievsky, known to all as The Steipler, and he grew up with the two families maintaining a close relationship. Before returning to war, Israel's mother asked him to go to The Steipler for a blessing. The Steipler, as most leaders in the Torah world, set hours where the public is welcome to visit and seek advice or a blessing without an appointment and of course without charge. Israel arrived prior to the time scheduled for the public so he would be able to return to his unit on schedule. When Israel knocked on The Steipler's door, he was told The Steipler was not feeling well and could not be disturbed. *Perfect*, he thought. *I did not want to bother The Steipler and at the same time I did what my mother asked of me.*

As he walked down the block, an assistant of The Steipler ran toward Israel and when he reached him, the assistant said, "The Steipler asked that I bring you to him."

Israel returned to The Steipler's door. As the elderly Steipler took my neighbor's hand, The Steipler shouted with tremendous intensity while pounding his hand on his *shtender* (book stand) "You shall return in good health and in one piece. You shall return in good health and in one piece. You shall return in good health and in one piece."

The soldier left trembling from the piercing words he had just heard. Nothing had ever made such a strong impression on him. He understood the repetition of the words "You shall return in good health and in one piece" three times to mean that he would return without physical harm, he would return without emotional harm, and he would return without spiritual harm.

As a tank commander and later a commander of a vehicle that went into enemy territory to rescue injured soldiers, he saw comrades die, become disfigured, break down mentally, and even lose their faith. But from the intensity of the blessing he had received, Israel knew he was coming home with his body, mind, and faith intact, and he did, thank G-d.

Israel Gurfinkel proudly served as a commander in Israel's army with courage and distinction. In the Israeli army, there is no such concept as "entitlement." On the contrary, the officers lead and place themselves in the most dangerous situations. Rather than entitlement there is responsibility.

My neighbor, Israel, also saw these examples in the greatest of Torah scholars whose greatness did not earn them comfort but on the contrary, the understanding that with greatness came the responsibility to advise, comfort, and teach others. He saw the greatest Torah scholars set aside many hours a week to be available to every person that sought their counsel or blessings and they did it without seeking remuneration.

It was the total converse of Rothstein's world. Gurfinkel, unlike Rothstein, is a true hero who cares about others. But, fortunately for most of us, as Edgar Watson Howe said, "A boy doesn't have to go to war to be a hero; he can say he doesn't like pie when he sees there isn't enough to go around."

How lucky we are that most of the time we are able help others without putting our life in harm's way. Sometimes, we need to just let a comment pass, set a person on the right path or extend a helping hand.

America also has brave servicemen and women who stand up to protect our freedom. Americans have served with courage and determination to protect liberty and to restore liberty to more places in the world than any other nation. America is great because Americans are willing to serve and to sacrifice for our country. These great Americans are not part of the "entitlement society." They are a part of the culture that puts their country and other people first. They do it because they love life and because other people are important.

John McCain said, "Serve a cause greater than oneself."

John F. Kennedy said, "Ask not what your country can do for you – ask what you can do for your country."

Rabbi Shapiro said, "Live with your heart on the right side."

All of these leaders stressed the same message and it is the message I learned growing up in my parents' home. A life well lived is measured by what one gives, not by what one gets.

Epilogue

SCOTT ROTHSTEIN remains in federal custody convicted of racketeering, money laundering, mail fraud, and two counts of wire fraud. Since he pled guilty to all charges, he faced up to 100 years behind bars. Rothstein's attorney argued thirty years would be an appropriate sentence and the prosecutor asked for forty years. On June 9, 2010, Judge Cohn sentenced Rothstein to fifty years in prison.

Before imposing the sentence, Judge Cohn stated "In its simplest form, this case is about the selling of fake financial products. The marketing, however, was anything but simple. It was sophisticated, rivaling that of Madison Avenue's advertising elite. It was all about image, wealth, power and influence, WPI." Judge Cohn went on to say "… Mr. Rothstein infiltrated so many spheres of public interest. He infiltrated so many parts of our daily lives – politics, sports, charities, law enforcement, the judiciary, the society page, TV commercials, the legal profession, billboards, [and] magazines.

Mr. Rothstein was seemingly omnipotent. He was everywhere. Not only was he everywhere, but he was everywhere with excesses." The Judge distinguished Rothstein's conduct from other Ponzi schemers pointing out "Mr. Rothstein created the fraudulent court orders in order to perpetuate the fraudulent scheme. These actions constitute the most egregious wrongs a licensed attorney can commit and represent a total disrespect for the authority and dignity of the courts. There can be no conduct more reviled than an attorney perpetrating such a fraud on the court."

That sentence may change, however, because there's one more line of work we can now attribute to Rothstein: FBI informant.

On March 16, 2010, a *Miami Herald* article written by Jay Weaver and Amy Sherman reported that Rothstein, as luck would have it, knew suspected mafia man, Roberto Settineri, through business dealings he had between the Versace mansion he owned an interest in and the security company he had hired for the mansion turned bed and breakfast. The article mentioned that the FBI was on Settineri's trail for three years but could not make a case. In walks Rothstein, when he returns from Morocco in November of 2009, with a wire, and the adventures of Rothstein take another twist. The entire world minus Settineri knew the FBI was watching Rothstein. Settineri allegedly took the bait and agreed to shred two boxes of Rothstein's documents and launder $79,000 for him. Bingo! He was ripe for arrest. On March 10, 2010, *SunSentinel.com* writer Jon Burstein indicated that "In Miami Beach, a FBI SWAT team arrested Roberto Settineri ...." With that feather in Rothstein's cap, he has reason to expect some consideration when it comes to reevaluating his sentence based upon assistance he provides the government. But with that adventure Rothstein will forever have an invisible target on his forehead that comes with turning in an alleged mafia man.

On March 15, 2010, Jim DeFede reporting for CBS4 I-Team stated, "Sources tell *CBS4 News* that because of his cooperation in this case, Rothstein will be entering the federal witness protection program – meaning he will serve his prison time for the Ponzi scheme under a different name and in a prison outside of Florida."

When the news broke, I shook my head in amazement at the man.

And the indictments continue to unfold. On April 27, 2010, Debra Villegas was charged with money laundering as part of Rothstein's scheme of deception. As reported on *SunSentinel.com*, "The charging document alleges that Villegas forged legal settlement agreements, which Rothstein sold to investors." On June 11,

2010, Debra Villegas admitted forging documents and pled guilty to conspiracy to commit money laundering. She faces up to ten years in prison.

She is cooperating with authorities in order to try and reduce her sentence, and such cooperation could result in additional indictments.

Be sure to visit me at www.EmpoweringLessons.com for updates. While you are there, share with the site's visitors valuable lessons you have learned and read what others did to make their lives more meaningful, full of the spirit of kindness and selflessness to which we should all aspire. I look forward to hearing your inspiring stories. Send your stories to me at stories@EmpoweringLessons.com.

Acknowledgments

FIRST, I thank the Creator of the World who has blessed me with this remarkable opportunity to write and publish a book. I am most grateful.

Next, I thank my neighbors whose stories inspired me to write this book. Their daily lives are full of acts of loving kindness towards others, and created the community that has had such an influence on who I am. Many of my neighbors did not want their names used out of modesty, but finally relented to my persistent requests, permitting me to use their stories with the hope that by my doing so, others might be inspired to perform thoughtful acts. Our community of North Miami Beach is a close warm community in which neighbors are friends, and I am grateful to be surrounded by such inspiring friends.

I would also like to thank:

— Joanna Gomez, who carefully and meticulously transcribed large sections of the manuscript.

— My son Yaacov, who, after a month-and-a-half in which I monopolized the family computer, asked in an act of compassion if he could read the manuscript. Yaacov offered many invaluable suggestions, and as each section was finished, he added his comments and recommendations, which helped me at a time when feedback was so essential. It is a special privilege to have such valuable and loving encouragement from one's own son.

— My mother, Ruth Sakowitz, who read my second draft and offered further helpful advice and direction. Her insights, guidance, and love have been a cherished blessing I have enjoyed my entire life.

— My rabbi, Rabbi Ephraim Eliyahu Shapiro, who has been a good friend and a source of great guidance to my family over the last twelve years. The book itself contains several of the beautiful lessons I absorbed from my rabbi's sermons over the years, and his insights clarified the themes of my story.

— Hannah Handler Hostyk, who offered regular feedback and encouragement on the manuscript while keeping the direction of the book focused and the story relevant.

— Barbara Lander, who further transformed the story into a more polished book and whose insights and recommendations helped the story shine through the pages.

— Michael Shilling, a lecturer at the University of Michigan, who provided the final editing and who did a masterful job by making the story more concise and refined. By suggesting the elimination of thirty stories about my community to allow for a more dynamic telling of the Rothstein saga, Michael has motivated me to write my next book, filled with stories that pierce the heart.

— Maurice Egozi, my business partner for more than fifteen years, who with his financial wizardry and knowledge, has joined me in analyzing each deal with which we are presented, not only for its potential earnings but also for the risk to our investors and in the end always acknowledging that, especially because our names are connected to our projects, we need to walk away from deals that are too good to be true.

— My wife, Leah, who gave me the emotional and physical space to devote myself to my writing over the past five months. During those months only a friend's wedding, an evening *Torah* class, or *Shabbos* could pry me from the keyboard during the evening. Leah's insights kept me focused on this book's main purpose, and confirmed how everything I have accomplished over the last almost twenty-five years is because of her. She has joyfully created a warm and tranquil home, anchoring me to be able to focus on outside business and community projects. Leah is an extraordinary woman and I am grateful for her vision and support.

— My children, Nechama Rivka, Yaacov Meir, Shira Devorah, Yael Adina, and Talia Chaya, whose devotion to helping others and each other has further inspired the words of this book. Your presence is in every story of loving kindness contained in this book.

— My final thanks go to my dear readers, for if they enjoy and benefit from my words, they will bring the pleasure I had writing *Miles Away ... Worlds Apart* to an even higher level.